DECCA AITKENHEAD is an award-winning journalist for the *Guardian* newspaper, where she interviews leading figures in public life. She lives in rural Kent with her two young sons.

Withdrawn Stock

BCP Libraries

Praise for *All At Sea*

'The sort of story people call "unputdownable" – a well-plotted, well-executed thriller. Except it's all heart-shatteringly true . . . Aitkenhead has an incredible gift for writing . . . Her ache for honesty is searing at times but the overwhelming truth is that Aitkenhead has produced a work of art'
Charlotte Edwardes, *Evening Standard*

'I finished it in one sitting – in a paralysed, stunned, empathetic trance . . . It is a beautifully written book. Were it not so devastating, it would be a joy to read . . . What makes the book powerful is that it reminds one that grief is about transformation, the loss of old moorings, a new permission to put the heart first – a sea change'
Kate Kellaway, *Observer*

'Agonising . . . This is a book entirely without sentimentality or rhapsodising . . . Aitkenhead's unblinking but resilient voice – sometimes stern, sometimes funny, always fierce – makes this book, like its author, inspiring in the best sense'
Claire Messud, *Guardian*

'What is left to the reader is gratitude to the writer for her honesty, lack of sentimentality, thoughtfulness and capacity to write spare, simple, beautiful prose. Decca Aitkenhead's loss was our gain'
David Aaronovitch, *The Times*

'An exemplary memoir . . . Acute, penetrating and at times extremely profound . . . However magnificent and powerful the book, you know it pales in comparison with the loss'
Helen Davies, *Sunday Times*

'An extraordinary memoir, a beautifully written account of life, love and what is left of both after tragedy . . . Utterly heart-breaking but it's also a brave and honest account of grief and its aftermath'
Mernie Gilmore, *Daily Express*

'This beautiful, brave and honest-to-the-very-core book describes exactly what Tony was like and how it feels like to have to go on without him. It's a remarkable work'
Eithne Farry, *Sunday Express*

'The book . . . ends with an image of her boys swimming again, back in J. . . *Spectator*

'Finely observed, emotionally truthful and beautifully written . . . testament to the extraordinary power of love that doesn't vanish when life of the beloved ends, but endures as long as memory itself'
Mail on Sunday

'Moving, insightful and wise, covering not only death, but life, love, motherhood and self identity. Anyone who's ever lost a loved one, or anyone who's ever lay awake at night worrying about anything will feel enlightened and comforted by Aitkenhead's truly brilliant writing'
The Pool

'Where *When Breath Becomes Air* offered a dying man's perspective on mortality, *All at Sea* offers a widow's perspective on survivor's guilt . . . Leaves you feeling unaccountably grateful – not only for your own relative serendipity, but for the wisdom borne of Aitkenhead's grit'
Washington Post

'A heart-wrenching tale of race, unlikely love, and how grief changes everything. It's unforgettable'
People

'No one who reads her brave and eloquent book will ever forget endearing Tony or their incandescent love story'
Boston Globe

'A surprising love story, searingly honest, a book of family, loss, death and ultimately life. A triumphant tour de force'
Eve Ensler

'An entrancing love story; a horrifying death story; a book about class, family, growing up, taking risks and learning how to be strong. Read it once, and it will be inside your head forever'
Andrew Marr

'Anyone who has loved, lost or grieved – that's all of us – should read it'
Alastair Campbell

'It brought a tear to my eye, and will be deeply empowering for those who read it'
Tanya Byron

'Unbearably moving and almost brutally compelling'   Adrian Chiles

'A remarkable story of sudden tragedy and grief. But it's about so much more than that. It's a powerful story of love and resilience'
Arianna Huffington

'A beautiful and painful guidebook through the taboo subject of death. Decca made me miss someone I've never met and, for today at least, savour those I love'
Russell Brand

all at sea

Decca
Aitkenhead

Withdrawn Stock
BCP Libraries

4th ESTATE • *London*

HarperCollins
PUBLISHERS
Since 1817

4th Estate
An imprint of HarperCollins*Publishers*
1 London Bridge Street
London SE1 9GF
www.4thEstate.co.uk

First published in Great Britain in 2016 by 4th Estate
This 4th Estate paperback edition published in 2017

1

Copyright © Decca Aitkenhead 2016

Decca Aitkenhead asserts the moral right to be
identified as the author of this work

A catalogue record for this book is available from the British Library

ISBN 978-0-00-814215-5

Typeset in Garamond and Bodoni Classico
Printed and bound in Great Britain by Clays Ltd, St Ives plc

All rights reserved. No part of this publication may be reproduced,
stored in a retrieval system, or transmitted, in any form or by any means,
electronic, mechanical, photocopying, recording or otherwise,
without the prior permission of the publishers.

This book is sold subject to the condition that it shall not, by way
of trade or otherwise, be lent, re-sold, hired out or otherwise circulated
without the publisher's prior consent in any form of binding or cover other
than that in which it is published and without a similar condition including
this condition being imposed on the subsequent purchaser.

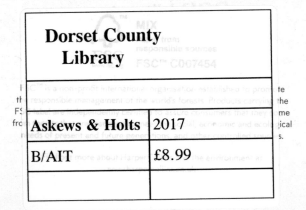

Dorset County Library	
Askews & Holts	2017
B/AIT	£8.99

For Tony

You always said I should write a book about you.
It wasn't meant to be this one.

prologue

The thing to remember about this story is that every word is true. If I never told it to a soul, and this book did not exist, it would not cease to be true. I don't mind at all if you forget this. The important thing is that I don't.

My three-year-old son asks me to tell him the story almost every day. 'Tell me the story about how Tony died-ed again,' he says. And so I do, until he knows the words and can join in, as if it were a well-worn nursery rhyme. He needs to hear the story to make it real for him. But the ritual makes it sound more like Little Red Riding Hood to me – just another fantastical fairy tale.

The first time I read the story of Tony's death, it was a news report in the *Guardian*, my own newspaper. I love newspapers. I have been a journalist for twenty years. Even as a child I was a compulsive writer, but only ever of diaries, letters, lists – never fiction. Where would be the point in making up a story, when the truth is by definition always more interesting? And so for twenty years I have been reading and writing what I thought of as the truth. Then I read about my own family's tragedy in my newspaper, and the only thing I could think was: they can't be talking about *me*. They can't mean *my* family. This could never happen to me and my family. This is something that happens to other people.

'This happens to other people' is a recurring cliché of the random tragedy survivor's experience. I have heard it countless times in my job, from stunned interviewees recounting a bolt from the blue – and to tell the truth, I have always found it puzzling. What do they mean? Why would they imagine that other people are any different from them? Now here I was, thinking exactly the same thing: this happens to other people. And slowly, I began to see why.

We read about freak disasters every day, knowing perfectly well that the news is not fiction. And yet, deep down, what we are reading must feel to us made up. Why else would we be so incredulous when they happen to us? Even the journalists who report them must be in the same boat. I have been writing about real people for all these years, and apparently had not grasped that they were real.

Back in the early Nineties, among a particular type of London media sophisticate, something called postmodernism was the height of fashion, and dinner parties would routinely be ruined by some cultural studies graduate boring everyone to death about the absurdity of constructs such as 'truth'. At the time I wrote it off as a fad for pseudo-intellectuals hoping to look clever. Now I wonder if they weren't onto something after all.

Because it isn't really possible to write about a real-life event without turning it into a form of fiction. Once an accident of chance has been organised into a narrative, it can be honest, and accurate, and illuminating. But it is only an edited version of a partial perspective, not the same thing as the truth.

So now I am afraid that by writing this story, I will make it untrue. Chapter headings and syntax and punctuation will elbow all my tears and grief out of the way, until the catastrophe has been reduced to just another piece of work, and my memories of what happened have been replaced by this printed version, creating a safe distance between myself and the horror.

Of course, in many ways this is enormously appealing. If I take control of this narrative and become its author, I will steal its power over me; I can detach myself from my own story, and escape. Who wouldn't want to do that? And yet, that is also the very thing I fear most.

For most of my life I have known how to control my feelings. I found that if you can control your feelings, you can pretty much control your whole world. It's amazingly effective. But Tony's death was beyond my control – and now, for the first time, so are my emotions. Tony always used to tell me to think less and feel more, but I never could. Now that that's all I can do, I can see he was right – and if feelings are his gift from the grave, I'm afraid of taming them into words.

But if I don't write about him, I am afraid I will forget too much. I was almost ten years old when my mother died, and I can remember someone telling me at the time to write down all my memories of her. What a daft idea, I remember thinking. Where would be the point? I'm hardly likely to forget anything about her. I remember all that very clearly. Unfortunately, however, within a remarkably short time I found I had forgotten almost everything else. She had been my mother for one week short of a decade, and before I was even in my teens I could barely remember a thing about her. I lost most of a decade of my life.

Tony drowned just a few months before our tenth anniversary, and I am frightened of losing that decade too. So I write because I don't want to forget.

1

'Just having coffee down on the beach,' Tony calls over his shoulder, as he strolls down the garden path towards the gate. Still half asleep, he treads languidly, flip-flops flapping faintly on the soles of his feet. Our three-year-old son, Joe, is playing inside in his bedroom, but I can't spot his older brother. From the front deck of the cottage, I call down to Tony.

'Have you got Jake?'

Tony settles on the edge of a sunlounger, his back to me, gazing out to sea. 'Yeah, got him here.' I look again, and there Jake is, in his navy blue pyjamas, playing in the sand between Tony's feet and the water's edge. It is just after 8 a.m. on a cloudless Caribbean morning.

We arrived here ten days ago, for a holiday that feels not

so much recreational as medicinal. Tony and I have two small children, two full-time jobs, and the usual unmanageable levels of exhaustion and stress. Twelve months earlier we moved out of London and launched into renovating a sixteenth-century farmhouse with the naïve excitement of a couple who had no idea what living in a building site with two little boys would be like. After an interminable winter of dust and rubble, we are frazzled. The holiday had been my idea. I know we can't afford to go away, I had said, but perhaps we can't afford not to either? I put the trip on a credit card, telling myself it was not an extravagance but a necessity.

I first came to this scruffy little fishing village on the south coast of Jamaica almost twenty years ago. Too remote and untamed for the package-holiday market, Treasure Beach is not a resort but just a dusty muddle of potholed lanes and driftwood shacks clustered around two bays, Calabash and Frenchman's. To the east and west, the coastline is wild and deserted. On the hillside overlooking the ocean, farmers grow scallion and melons in blood-red soil.

I was first sent here to write a travel story about a new hotel called Jake's. Back then, in the early Nineties, Jake's was nothing more than a few artfully rustic cottages nestled in a rocky cove between the village's two beaches. But it is owned by a family of celebrated Jamaican filmmakers and artists, and over the years evolved into a boutique spa hotel with a boho hipster reputation among fashionable types who find St Barts and Barbados a bit bling, and prefer not to be bothered by paparazzi stalking Simon Cowell. Treasure Beach's other guesthouses attract a more hippyish backpacker type, but even in high season tourists seldom outnumber the battered wooden fishing boats on the beach.

Almost two decades later, Treasure Beach feels more like home to me than anywhere else on earth. I have been coming here every year, beguiled by the discovery of epic melodrama concealed beneath its sleepy surface. This tiny Caribbean community contains more comedy and intrigue than I have ever managed to find in London. In 2000 I rented a house in Calabash Bay for nine months while I wrote a book, and some of my oldest and most precious friendships belong here in this village.

After all these years, Calabash beach is as familiar to me as my own reflection. It is a slender curl of sand between two rocky points no more than 300 yards apart, dotted with just seven cottages and villas. Over time I have stayed in all but one of the houses, and for this holiday we have rented the cottage at the eastern end of the bay, close to the corner where the fishing boats lie upturned on the sand. It is the cottage where Tony and I stayed the very first time I brought him here.

Before our boys were born, holidays involved late nights in local bars, sleeping until noon beneath the cool of a ceiling fan and lazing afternoons away in a hammock. Those days are long gone. Dusk falls fast in the tropics; it is inky black by 7.30 p.m., and on this holiday we have all been in bed not much later. Most mornings I have been on the tennis court at dawn with my friend Annabelle, a ballsy six-foot motorbiker, while Tony wandered down to the fishing boats with the boys to see what the night catch had brought. We have been laughing at what an unexpectedly wholesome couple we appear to have become.

'Isn't it funny,' Tony had remarked after the first few days, 'how this is actually more fun than everything we used to get up to here?' We are slowly beginning to unwind, to feel almost normal again. I am even going to give yoga a go. For years everyone has been telling me to try it, and at last I am about to; my first lesson starts at 9 a.m. at Jake's. Feeling self-conscious about how creaky I have become, I had been stretching on the deck when a friend appeared in the garden, passing by on his way into the village.

Shugoo is a chef, and one of Tony's closest friends in the village. A great mountain of a man, he is practically round, and on first impression can appear rather solemn – even Buddha-like – for he tends to move majestically slowly, and is at ease in silence. But when Shugoo laughs, he explodes into peals of schoolboy giggles, and he and Tony are usually helpless with laughter within minutes together. The kettle had just boiled, so Tony made coffee, and the pair wandered down to the beach to leave me to my stretching.

The only yoga move I have ever tried is something very basic called a sun salutation. A friend showed me it years ago, and I'm pretty sure I don't do it properly, but I bend backwards and begin. Sunlight dapples the deck through the tangled branches of an overhanging calabash tree. I straighten and lean forward to touch my toes. Any second now our son Joe will emerge onto the deck and demand we join the others on the beach, but for now all is quiet, and in the rare calm my mind drifts.

As I straighten a few minutes later and stand, my eye catches something in the sea. A head is bobbing in the water. The swimmer is clearly out of their depth – but how is that possible? The swimmer can be no more than 10 feet from the shore. On a normal day you can wade out 30 or 40 feet before your feet no longer touch the bottom. It must be a child, I think idly – a very small child. I scan the beach, wondering where its parents can be.

The waves on Frenchman's beach can often be fierce, but Calabash Bay has been like a millpond since we arrived. We have spent hours in the ocean most days, the boys astonished by the crystal warmth of glassy water. 'Dec it's like a giant bath!' they would squeal. 'Look, Tony, we can see our toenails!' They call us by our names instead of Mum and Dad, and it makes others on the beach laugh. We had planned to move to another cottage around the headland for the second week of our holiday, but this beach is so perfect for the children that we cancelled the other booking and decided to stay put here.

The villa to our left belongs to friends, and when guests had left the previous day the owners had let our boys use the pool. Jake is four, and on the cusp of learning to swim; he had spent the whole day in the pool with Tony, splashing about without his floatation vest. Tony had taught him how to tread water, and Jake was elated with his new buoyancy.

That afternoon, while they had been in the pool, I had glanced out to sea and saw the current had shifted. The bay was still fairly calm but a little choppy, no longer glassy. To anyone unfamiliar with these waters, the change would be imperceptible, but I understood its significance. Beneath an apparently benign surface, a treacherous undertow builds, doubling the depth of the water and sucking anyone in it out to sea. I have been caught in one a few times here, and the force can be startling. 'See how the current's changed?' I had called to Tony, gesturing out to sea. He had cast a brief glance, but could see nothing, and had turned back to Jake. We had this lovely pool to ourselves, so it seemed unimportant, and soon drifted out of my mind.

Now I take another look at the head bobbing in the water. It is only seconds since I spotted it, but already it has moved further from the shore. I scan the beach again, looking for Tony, when a sudden idea shocks me. My gaze snaps back to the swimmer. That can't be Jake, can it? Surely not. No, Tony would never allow him into the sea by himself. Besides, without his floatation vest on Jake can't swim. I stare again. Bloody hell, it *is* Jake. Is it? I squint, shielding my eyes from the sun. It can't be. But yes, I think it is.

He didn't take his vest down to the beach, did he? He must have. But he was still in his pyjamas. And Tony let him go swimming by himself? Tony is normally quite jumpy around water; he has never been a good swimmer, and is easily panicked when the boys are in the sea. I wonder what they can be up to. Vaguely uneasy, I turn and glance around the deck. Swimming costumes and beach towels and sarongs are slung over backs of chairs. I see suntan lotion and straw hats scattered on the floor. I spot Joe's swimming vest hooked over a branch of the calabash tree, where I had hung it out to dry the night before. And then I freeze. I am staring at Jake's vest. He cannot be wearing it, because it is right there next to Joe's in the tree.

I'm flying down the garden path to the beach before my mind has time to calibrate the drama. That is Jake out there in the ocean, and he cannot swim. The panic flooding me is unlike anything I have ever known. But even as I sprint I can't quite seriously believe in my own fright. Surely this can't be a genuine emergency, can it? In real life, emergencies always turn out to be false alarms – and this one is palpably implausible. Jake is still only yards from the shore, after all. We are on holiday. I know this beach inside out.

But I don't stop running. Within seconds I am through the gate and onto the sand. I don't take my eyes off Jake. But then I see that Tony is already ahead of me, ploughing through the water towards him. Within moments he has our son in his hands, and lifts the spluttering child out of the waves above his head. Jake coughs and chokes, catches his breath, and relaxes in Tony's arms. The crisis is over. Tony wraps an arm around Jake and starts to head back to shore.

As I sink onto the sand to watch, the relief makes me giggly. Oh dear, I think, we are never going to hear the end of this. Tony is such a drama queen about water, he's going to blather on about this all day. By teatime he will probably be claiming the waves were 6 feet high. Tony loves an anecdote, and this one is right up his street. Oh well, I smile. It may even be the highlight of his holiday.

But something is wrong. Tony and Jake are now vertical in the water, facing each other, submerged up to their chins. Although not far from the shore, Tony is already out of his depth. Waves are breaking in their faces; they are struggling to stay afloat. What can be the matter? And then I see. Tony can't manage to swim holding Jake. He can barely keep both of them afloat, let alone get them back to shore.

I leap to my feet and scramble into the water. Within moments I am out of my depth, but the swell is gentle and it doesn't occur to me to feel anything other than purposeful calm as I swim. Because really, what is there to worry about now? They are not terribly far away. I will just take Jake, swim him back to shore, and once Tony can use both arms he will follow.

If anything, what I feel as I swim towards them is mild embarrassment. I hadn't considered pausing to undress, but haring into the ocean with all my clothes on now strikes me as mildly melodramatic. I hope no one was looking. The only other person I'm aware of on the beach is Shugoo, and he will probably tease me all morning about my Baywatch antics.

Tony and I say nothing to each other when I reach them. We are both focused on Jake. Tony passes him to me, I flip him onto his back, twist onto my back beneath him, cup his chin in my left hand, and with my right hand begin to swim for shore. It's surprisingly easy. My chief memories of school swimming lessons in the Eighties recall the shame of ill-fitting swimwear, and the malice of our swimming teacher. But now I find that I can also remember the basics of lifesaving. It is thirty years since I was shown the ropes, and I have had no cause to practise since then, but evidently it must be like riding a bike. I will have Jake back on the beach in no time.

There is a nervy moment when Jake wriggles out of my arm. 'I want to face you!' he protests, twisting onto his front, and at once we start to sink. Suddenly I am as helpless as Tony had been. 'No, Jake! You have to lie on your back! This is not a game!' I don't know if my scream frightened him, but he flips onto his back obediently, and once again we are swimming.

I am not sure how long we have been in the water when I turn to see the beach, but it feels like quite a while. A surprisingly long time, in fact. Surely by now we should be there? I twist my neck to look – and cannot believe what I see.

This can't be possible. The beach should be just a few feet away. But we are nowhere near it; we're not even halfway there. What is going on? I remember the undertow. Of course, that's what's going on. How could I have forgotten? We are trapped in its current. But it is nothing like any undertow I have ever known before. This feels more like the force of a gigantic magnet sucking us out to the horizon. And yet, even now, it does not cross my mind to panic.

I will just have to swim harder, I tell myself, and it is going to take a little longer than I had thought.

It still has not occurred to me to worry when I spot another head nearby in the water. The head turns and I see that it is Blouser, a fisherman I've known for fifteen years. He must be in his forties by now, but is still lean and fearsomely fit; his home is a tin shack on the beach near our cottage, and he more or less lives in the sea. We have bought fish from Blouser most days on this holiday, and Jake and Joe have been dazzled and fascinated by him, for he can sometimes seem more amphibian than human.

I open my mouth to call to him, but his expression silences me. Blouser looks frightened to death. He stares back at me across the water, his features rigid with terror and exhaustion.

What is going on? Why does Blouser look like that? What has happened? 'Blouser!' I shout. 'Are you okay?' He struggles to nod. 'Can you take my hand?' I yell, and he does. We swim together for a few yards, until I see his features relax. 'Blouser, are you standing? Are you in your depth?' He nods faintly, head tilted back, straining to keep his mouth above water. I swim on another yard or so past him, searching with outstretched toes until at last they touch wet sand. Hoisting Jake above my shoulders, weak with fatigue, I carry him out of the waves, lower him to his feet, and together we fall to our knees.

'Are you alright?' I gasp. Jake blinks back at me and grins. 'Yeah, fine.' Brushing sand off his pyjamas, he shrugs away the adventure as if it were nothing.

As I kneel and catch my breath I'm inclined to think he is probably right. There were a couple of dicey moments out there, certainly, and I am very glad it's over. But nothing significantly dangerous happened. Jake just got out of his depth, and needed help getting in. I don't know why Blouser looked so panic-stricken, but now that Jake is safely ashore he must be fine. I stand and turn to look for him on the beach, anticipating a hug and rueful smiles.

But I don't see Blouser. I don't even look for him. As I stand and turn, what I see makes me forget all about Blouser. Tony should be wading onto the beach by now; at worst he should be back in his depth. But Tony isn't anywhere near the shore. He isn't even where I left him. He is further out to sea, much, much further, 50 feet off shore, and isn't even trying to swim.

He is tipping backwards in the water, his neck lolling in the swell, as if the waves were an armchair. He raises an arm, but the gesture looks half-hearted, almost casual, and a moment later he lets it drop. He is shouting something, but the voice is not his. It sounds slurred and thick, more animal than human. 'Help,' I hear. 'Help.' But there is no urgency in his cry.

What is he doing all the way out there? Without thinking I race back into the water. A voice from the beach halts me. 'No!' Waist-deep in surf, I turn. Blouser is shouting, and his pitch of raw fear seizes me for long enough to turn again and register three men out in the ocean, yards from Tony, swimming hard towards him. One is Shugoo; I can't make out the other two. But whoever they are, they are going to reach Tony long before I can. I wade back to the beach.

It's at this moment that time's rhythm becomes un-recognisable, simultaneously frenetic and slow-motion. Seconds begin to stretch like minutes, minutes feel more like hours. Time is passing, but nothing is happening, nothing is changing. Tony is still floundering in the waves, the swimmers still have not reached him. I am pacing frantically, pointing and shouting in confusion. Why are they dawdling? Can't they see he's in trouble?

'Go to Tony!' I scream, waving my arms. 'Help him! For God's sake, can't you see he's drowning?' Is he? I am shocked by what has just come out of my mouth. He can't literally be drowning, can he? I am being hysterical. But the hysteria in my voice has unnerved me even more than my words. Is that really what is actually happening? Tony is drowning? That's absurd; it's not possible. But Christ, can't they just hurry up and get to him?

People are streaming out of houses all along the beach. I see Michael, a friend who works in the guesthouse to our right, sprint into the water and fling a float attached to a rope – but the onshore breeze blows it back to his feet. Damian, another friend who works in the villa to our left, comes flying down the bank from the pool and hurls a life ring out to sea, but again the wind blows it back. As each rescue attempt flops, the scene begins to look like some sort of surreal slapstick pantomime; we are cartoonish in our frantic helplessness. For a fleeting moment I actually cringe, mortified to be the cause of such a public spectacle.

Because obviously Tony is going to be alright. For all the drama, he hasn't actually gone under. The swimmers will reach him any second now, and in half an hour he will be drinking a Red Stripe and complaining about sand in his ears.

I am right. The swimmers do get to him. Somehow they have Michael's float in their hand, and Michael is holding his end of the rope. The three men cluster around the float with Tony in their arms, and Michael stands in the surf and pulls. I take the rope in front of him, like a two-person tug-of-war team, and together we haul them ashore.

It is over. The panic has exhausted its jeopardy. Michael and I drag Tony onto the sand, and for the first time since I carried Jake out of the ocean I remember him. Now that Tony is safe, I turn my attention to our son. 'Sweetheart, are you okay?'

He has not moved from the spot where I left him, and is sitting with legs outstretched, squirming. His hands rake the sand. 'No.' He is staring past my legs at his father, wide-eyed and white, his voice thin with anxiety. 'No, I'm worried about Tony.' I turn, expecting to see Tony sitting up. But he isn't. His eyes aren't even open. He is just lying there.

What? For a fraction of a second I'm confused. Then I think I understand. Oh Tony, I think, I know this was a proper scare – but there's no need to ham it up and spin it out for the sake of the anecdote. Come on, Tone. Just sit up and open your eyes now so we can go back to being on holiday.

'Dec,' Jake says behind me. I turn back to look at him. 'What's that white stuff coming out of Tony's nose?'

And then I see it. From each nostril, snaking down to his chin, trickles a stream of white foam. It looks like whipped egg white. I stare at it in shock. I have no idea what that foam is, or what it signifies. I am not a doctor. But even I can see it looks sinister, and dread begins to wrap itself around me.

Don't be ridiculous, I tell myself. He probably just needs to vomit up a bucketload of seawater. But still Tony doesn't move. I want to scream at him, 'Wake up! A joke's a joke, now wake the fuck up!' But Jake is at my side, and Tony is surrounded by a semicircle of men, one of whom is kneeling over him and appears to be administering CPR. Tony really is unconscious. But he's going to come round any moment. It's just that the process will be messier than I had imagined. It is probably best, I think, if Jake does not watch.

'Let's go back up to the cottage and find Joe,' I suggest lightly, taking his hand. 'Joe's probably wondering where we've got to.' I lead Jake up the path back to the cottage, and find Joe on the deck, leaning over the railings, straining to see the commotion on the beach.

'Is Tony going to be okay?' Jake asks. 'I think so,' I say brightly, but even I can hear how brittle my breeziness sounds. 'I think the doctors will come and make him better.' Struggling to appear calm, I make my way into our bedroom to search for my phone. I think I have found it until I try to make a call and realise I am stabbing wildly at an iPod. By the time I locate my phone and call Jake's, my fingers are shaking and I misdial twice before getting through.

A receptionist answers the phone with what feels like the longest greeting in the history of the hospitality industry: 'Hello, this is Colleen speaking, welcome to Jake's hotel in Treasure Beach. How may I direct your call?' Before she can get it all out I hear myself screaming, 'Send help now! Tony has been pulled from the water. He is unconscious. Send help now! Send someone, now!' I hang up in a blur of shock, worried that I will have frightened Jake and Joe, embarrassed about sounding deranged, afraid that I will have caused an unnecessary fuss, and scared that help will not arrive in time.

'We want to see Tony,' Joe says. 'Can we go and see him?' I don't know what to do, but think he must have come round by now, and the sooner the boys can see that he is fine the better. I take them by the hand and together we walk back down the path to the beach.

Where did all these people come from? Half an hour ago the beach had been deserted; now it looks like a carnival. People are streaming in from every direction; they are pouring through our garden, down the lane, along the beach. As we reach the gate I spot my friend Annabelle racing across the sand and falling to her knees beside Tony. Oh thank God, I think. Annabelle has medical training. Now that Annabelle is here, everything is going to be alright.

With Jake in one hand and Joe in the other, I lead them

past the crowds and down to the water's edge. From here we can see Annabelle's back as she kneels over Tony. She knows what she is doing. Any second now he is going to throw up and come round; it can only be a matter of time. Someone in the crowd shouts at me, 'Get your car keys, take him to the doctor!' But the nearest hospital is half an hour away; how is that going to help?

As we stand and watch, warm waves lapping at our ankles, my mind allows just one horrifying thought. What if Tony has been unconscious for so long that when he comes round he will be brain-damaged? Please God no. This idea is so unthinkably shocking that when I see Annabelle press two fingers to his neck, it takes me a moment to register the significance. I stare, bewildered. Why is she checking for a pulse?

Annabelle's fingers remain pressed to his neck. Then she looks up at the ring of faces gazing down at Tony and slowly shakes her head. I watch in disbelief. Is this some sort of joke? I keep staring, stunned. No. No no no no.

'Let's go back up to the cottage,' I hear myself say, and lead the boys past the crowd towards the garden gate. Suddenly we feel quite peripheral to the drama; we slip quietly away, as if this scene on the beach, this unfolding catastrophe, has nothing to do with us at all. And in my mind, it almost hasn't. What they all think is happening here right now cannot be true; it is not happening. We climb the path together in silence. I am too dazed to form words. As we enter the cottage a figure races past the open kitchen window and I hear him say 'Him dead', but still I do not believe it. They are wrong. In a minute Annabelle is going to come and tell us Tony is conscious and fine.

'Will Tony be okay?' asks one of the boys. 'I hope so,' I reply. 'I think a doctor is on his way.' I look at them, and see that Jake is still in his pyjamas. They are caked in sand.

'Let's go and wash all this sand off,' I suggest, and as if in a dream I lead them into the bathroom. We are going to do something normal; it is going to make everything normal. I perch on the edge of the bath, and turn on the shower. Water explodes everywhere, drenching me. As I wrestle with the shower head I register the silence of boys who would ordinarily fall about at such comedic misfortune. I look up from the edge of the bath to the door and see Annabelle standing in the door frame. She gazes straight at me, unsmiling, and very slowly shakes her head.

I stumble into her arms. 'No!' I am shouting at her. She holds me tightly; I cannot stand. I lurch back, staring at her face, willing her to say I have misunderstood. 'Dec,' Jake says softly. He stares up at me, frightened. 'Why is your face like that? What's happening?' I open my mouth, but no sound comes out. Joe wraps his arm around my leg and peers up anxiously. 'Has Tony died-ed?' he asks.

I look down at my children. 'Yes. Yes, he has. Tony has died.'

2

My memories of the days before Tony drowned must be unreliable, because in my mind they resemble the opening scenes of a cheap horror film. Every moment now seems so laced with menacing pathos that our oblivion to what was coming feels scarcely plausible. But when we sat side by side on the very spot where Tony would lie dead twenty-four hours later, how could we have known it was our last day together? We thought we had all the time in the world.

'Do you think,' Tony had mused idly, 'our boys will bring their own kids here one day?' I lay back on the sand, his hand in mine, and smiled up at the sky. 'I've never thought of that, Tone. But now you say it, yeah. I hope they do. What an amazing idea.'

The truth was, I had never imagined we would bring our own kids to Treasure Beach. I hadn't seriously expected us to make it as a couple, or have children of our own to take anywhere. If someone had told me ten years earlier that one day we would lie on Calabash beach and watch our sons build sandcastles while we speculated about grandchildren, I would have told them they were out of their mind.

When Tony and I first met, I was married to a man I loved very much. Everyone loved Paul. Everyone loved our marriage. We were one of those couples who make people sentimental; the sort that serves as a repository for their faith in the dreamy ideal of happily ever after. I loved being that couple.

Before then the only kind of couple I had ever been involved with was of the strictly comedy variety. Most of my friends had been falling madly in and out of love for years, and appeared to have no difficulty finding partners with whom they could contemplate a future, but the boyfriends I chose would have been impossible to mistake for credible candidates. There was the flatteringly pretty drummer who lived with his parents and wrote terrible poetry, and a morose Irish chef from Derry, whose appeal would have been indiscernible had I not been immature enough to find any whiff of the IRA romantic. He taught me how to say Tiocfaidh ár lá – our day will come – and I was thrilled. There was a postman, a DJ, a sales rep, a bouncer – and I was fond of them all. Falling in love with any of these men, however, would have been demonstrably absurd.

I was reasonably content with the comedy boyfriends, because it felt unrealistic to expect to meet a serious one. I don't think this assumption was subjected to close analysis at the time, but the problem would have been easy enough to identify. Losing one's heart to someone requires a degree of recognition – a shared sensibility – and this was hard to find in anyone else when my childhood had left me marooned between all recognisable categories of social class. In the dating game I was a stateless refugee.

My parents had met at Dartington Hall in the 1950s, when it was still a progressive boarding school favoured by middle-class radicals. Black and white photographs show them as teenagers marching to Aldermaston, wearing CND badges, smoking roll-ups. My father's father had been a conscientious objector; my mother's father was an Oxford don. They married before she turned twenty-one, and moved to Bristol; he became a teacher, and at twenty-three she gave birth to her first son. After their second arrived they moved to rural Wiltshire, to a broken-down cottage in a tiny hamlet of woodland and old watermills. A third son was born in their bedroom, and my father gave up teaching to become a carpenter. They were still in their twenties when I arrived in 1971.

Because I am reasonably well-spoken, these days people often assume I come from money. When I was a child, however, we would get mistaken for hippies. To Tory Wiltshire in the Seventies, CND car stickers and a subscription to the *Guardian* were enough to consign a family's reputation to the outlandish extremes of bohemia, but this was no more accurate than the false impression of wealth. My parents had little patience with the lazy hypocrisies of hippies – nor did they have any money.

We didn't have a television, either, but this was unrelated to having no money. It was a signifier of the particular social category to which my parents belonged – one that was very much of its time, relying as it did on the possibility of living in a big house in the country without earning very much. In essence, it meant being highly educated, intellectually radical but indifferent to materialism. My father used to half-joke that we were the 'genteel poor', meaning we didn't care about money. We didn't care about fashion, or cars, or appearances. What we cared about were words. Conversation wasn't just a worthy substitute for material possessions, such as a television, but a superior currency of limitless value – the supreme, unrivalled expression of love.

As a consequence, we were an extremely noisy family. When I think about family mealtimes now, in my head I hear something like a cross between *The Moral Maze* and *Question Time*. Even *The Moral Maze*'s smug undertones are faintly audible, for while we were all shouting away about God or Denis Healey, I think we shared an unspoken understanding that this was a dialogue from which other children expected to be excluded. Other children didn't know about the Labour party, had no idea religion was man-made, and were not typically solicited for their opinions on the monarchy. How we knew this I could not say, but I am sure we did.

We called our parents by their names instead of Mum and Dad. Prefixes for relatives – uncle this or aunt that – were considered infra dig, as were the euphemisms conventionally deployed for bodily parts and functions. 'Waterworks' or 'down below' made us squirm with laughter. Swear words, on the other hand, were entirely acceptable; we swore like troopers as soon as we could talk, and had to be coached in the delicate diplomacy of who would and would not find this offensive. The distinction was surprisingly easy to grasp, though occasionally its subtleties would fox us. 'It's alright!' we would bellow across a crowded room at our mother. 'I was *going* to say fuck – but I didn't.'

This hybrid identity our parents fashioned for us was probably recognisable to their Sixties generation. By the Eighties, however, its combination of entitlement, coarseness, penury and privilege made no sense at all to the other kids at our local comprehensive. When I Tippexed my Remembrance Sunday poppy white, the pacifist protest was widely interpreted to signify lesbianism. My refusal to accept the school maths cup was intended as a winning egalitarian gesture, but received as further evidence that I was 'up 'erself' and weird. Our father's Scottishness only made matters worse. Although born and bred in England, we were indoctrinated to regard England – and worst of all, London – with deep suspicion, and our contempt for every national occasion of patriotic unity – a royal wedding, the world cup, Tim Henman doing quite well at Wimbledon – only exiled us further. The only other people I knew who occupied our peculiarly niche substratum of the British class system were members of my extended family.

My teenage self was pragmatic enough to take pride in our failure to fit in. When I left home, the wilful isolation still did not present an immediate problem. Or rather, a solution presented itself before it had begun to dawn on me that I might need one. Very early on as an undergraduate in Manchester, I stumbled upon the city's gay village, and spent the entirety of my student years blissfully within its confines. Given that I am straight, I did sometimes wonder why. Looking back, it is obvious. Gay culture represented a social universe in which class had been trumped by sexuality, and everyone shared my own sense of being an outsider.

But when I graduated and moved to London to begin a career in journalism, class identity became an unavoidable issue. I thought it highly unlikely that I would fall in love with a man who did not read books or watch *Newsnight*, but could not see myself getting into bed with anyone called Hugo – and was seldom invited to anyway. The Hugos found me puzzling, and were understandably put off by my unaccountable prejudice against perfectly nice things like rugby and good wine. Sometimes I would find myself at a Notting Hill house party full of privately educated young professionals, and wonder how they could tell each other apart. As far as I could see, at the end of the night they could couple up and go home with anyone, and it would probably work out fine. Part of me pitied their interchangeability. Another part coveted the clarity of identity, because it seemed to make falling in love so enviably straightforward.

Paul was photographing Tony Blair at the 1997 Labour party conference when a mutual friend introduced us. A few hours later we met up in a bar to watch Celtic play football, and by the time I went to bed that night I was in love. It was as easy as that.

A working-class Glaswegian, Paul had joined the Labour party at fifteen, and credited politics with firing up an ambition to escape his Glasgow tenement and defy his alcoholic father's order to quit education and train as a glazier. He went to college, became a photographer, moved south, joined Reuters, won awards, and by the time we met was an established member of the London media scene.

He looked like a young Paul Newman, but his car was knee-deep in empty cheese and onion crisp packets, the back seats buried beneath a mountain of unpaid parking tickets. On assignment he would not always bother to pack clothes. When the ones he was wearing became too filthy to work in, he would nip into the nearest branch of Next, undress in a cubicle, ask an assistant to fetch a new outfit, put it on, leave the old one behind and go on his way without pausing to glance in a mirror. He could recite Robert Burns poetry, but swore so liberally that even cunt could be deployed by Paul as a casual term of affection. 'He's a lovely cunt,' he would often say fondly of a friend. Nice London girlfriends found all of this bewildering. But I had found a fellow refugee, and the rush of recognition was electrifying.

On our first proper date I took him home to meet my

father. In retrospect I can see this was odd, but at the time it felt perfectly natural. When I picture myself presenting Paul to him now, I'm reminded of our old childhood cat trotting down the drive with a rabbit swinging from her jaws. She would drop her kill on the doormat, sit beside it triumphantly, and yowl for one of us to come and admire how clever she had been. From the sofa in my father's living room, glowing, I watched my new boyfriend enchant him. They talked about football and politics. The framed Declaration of Arbroath which hung in the hallway, asserting Scotland's independence in 1320, was not something Paul had ever expected to find in a country house in Wiltshire, and he was spellbound. Within a week he had moved in with me.

We were happy beyond our wildest dreams. We bought a flat together in Hackney, and threw fabulous parties; he took me to the Highlands, I took him to Treasure Beach. After just eighteen months we got married on my grandmother's farm in Scotland. He wore a kilt, I wore bunches; it was, by universal consent, a magical wedding. Six months later we set off around the world.

Our working lives in London had been leaving us with only the scrag end of each day to ourselves, and we wanted more time together, so I cooked up an idea to write a travel book which would take us around the globe, ending up in Treasure Beach, where we lived for nine months while I wrote it. The return home to real life was a little bumpy, but everyone said that was only to be expected. In 2003 we moved to a beautiful big Victorian house on

Ainsworth Road in Hackney, where we would in theory begin the next chapter of our charmed life and start a family. The only downside in it all was that by then we were both miserable.

The disintegration of a marriage is so excruciatingly complicated that to extract any definitive cause from the carnage would be trite – and yet it is what we all do. The most commonly cited explanation for the breakdown of a relationship is the terrible realisation, on both sides, that each person is not whom the other had thought. In our case, if I had to name one reason, it would not be that. It was more that Paul and I had been wrong about who we ourselves were.

I had been intoxicated by Paul's indifference to trad-itional middle-class preferences for domestic order, finan-cial prudence, responsible drinking. Over time it became increasingly apparent that, actually, these mattered more to me than I had liked to think. In Paul they triggered such primal hostility that the only way he could see to remain loyal to his roots was to systematically sabotage the very life his ambition had longed for and led him to. For him, self-preservation was English and prissy; integrity and honour lay in self-destruction. He could never quite decide where he belonged. Was it in professional London's high-ceilinged kitchens eating fettuccine, or on a park bench in Glasgow drinking Special Brew? I wanted the fantasy of a husband who would observe the conventions of a comfortable life, without in any way acting like every other middle-class bore. We could see it was hopeless. We did not know what to do. So we struggled on, trapped in the hell of loving someone who filled us with dismay and despair.

If Ainsworth Road had been a typical London street where no one knows their neighbours, we might never have met Tony. But traffic controls at one end of the road made it feel more like a cul de sac, and within a few months of moving in we became friendly with the tall, gregarious, good-looking mixed-race man with dreadlocks who was always out on the pavement and seemed to know everyone. He was so loud you could hardly miss him. He lived with his wife and their ten-year-old daughter, and in the interests of appearances owned a property development company. He had a geezerish air of mischief about him, but came across as such a happy-go-lucky family man that you would never have guessed he wholesaled cocaine for a living and was addicted to crack.

At first we would just say hello in passing on the street. As we got to know him better, he would sometimes drop in. He was always smiley, and invariably had an anecdote, which he would tell at breakneck speed in his booming gravelly baritone, the accent a curious combination of flat Yorkshire vowels and cockney glottal stops. When animated – as he usually was – he had an endearing tendency to tumble his words together into a flurried blur, and sentences would frequently end with 'Know wha' I mean?' The question was rhetorical, but quite often I didn't.

It was hard to judge his self-assurance. He was a physically arresting presence, six foot two and muscular with a purposeful stride, his broad shoulders accentuated by good posture. He carried his head unusually high, and stood square. The dreadlocks weren't braided but left to form naturally, and fell shoulder-length; he wore them tied back in a scrunchie, and would toss the fringe out of his eyes with a faint shake. Always holding a spliff, he smelt of designer cologne and cannabis. He dressed casually but expensively – Armani jeans, Phat Farm sweatshirts, white trainers – and although in his late thirties would sometimes be mistaken for a professional footballer. The initial impression was of lively confidence, but as we got to know him better I began to wonder. There was something in his expression to suggest bashful uncertainty about his place, and the loudness might be camouflage for doubt.

Tony and his family moved out of Ainsworth Road the following year, to a house further east. He still appeared on the street regularly, though, and when our rental flat needed to be redecorated we asked him to put his property company's team on the job. Paul was away working in Afghanistan while the work was being done. Tony would pop in with progress reports, or a query about a detail, and when he appeared one evening with a bottle of wine we sat up late talking.

By now I was curious about his life, because he had dropped enough hints to suggest it might contain something of a story. Like any career criminal, Tony had been dissembling and obfuscating for most of it, and was adept at deflecting direct inquiry – but I am equally adept at being nosey. At first my questions made him so uncomfortable that he would literally squirm in his chair. Before long the tenacity of my interest disarmed and then enthralled him. 'Are you trying to interview me?' he would tease, and in a way I suppose I was. His visits became more frequent, and over the course of late-night conversations at my kitchen table I learnt the story of his life – or at least, the one he chose to tell.

Tony was born in Leeds in 1965, to a white fifteen-year-old mother. He had a hazy memory of being told that her father was a policeman, but whether this was true he did not know. Of his own father he knew nothing. When Tony was a toddler there had been some speculation that he might be half-Persian, but as he grew older it became evident that his ethnic origins were African or Caribbean. He liked to think his father had been visiting the UK from Africa as a student – even a Nigerian prince, possibly – but conceded that a black man in Leeds in 1965 was more likely to have belonged to the post-war Windrush generation of West Indian immigrants. Whether the man had ever been made aware of his son's existence was unknown. Tony preferred to hope he had not, and could be absolved of blame for abandoning him.

The first eighteen months of his life were a mystery. He did not know for how long he remained with his mother, and thought he might at one stage have been a Barnardo's baby. All he knew was that at the age of 18 months he was fostered by a white family who lived in a suburb on the outskirts of Leeds. His earliest memory was of rocking frantically in bed at night to soothe himself.

The Wilkinsons already had three older children of their own, two boys and a girl. They were in most respects a conventional upper working-class white couple – he was an engineer, she a housewife who later worked in Debenhams – but they had fostered more than 100 children before Tony arrived, many of them troubled or abused, and several black. Tony never fully understood why he was the one they decided to adopt, but within a few years he was Tony Wilkinson.

Tony had two versions of his childhood. Sometimes he was the unaccountably deviant cuckoo in the nest of a decent and law-abiding family, undeserving of their love for an adoptive son hell-bent on causing trouble. More often he was the damaged victim of racism so institutionalised in Yorkshire in the Seventies that his only option for survival was violence and crime. In either account, the youth criminal justice system subjected Tony to every punishment it could think of – borstal, secure children's homes, youth detention, the short sharp shock.

He always maintained that he burgled his first house at the age of four. It sounded impossible, but he was adamant. He stole everything he could get his hands on, and his father had to fit a lock on every bedroom door except his. His mother, he said with a smile, was a terrific snob, and forbade him to walk through the local council estate, unaware that he had already been barred from almost every house. Expelled from four primary schools, he became an accomplished truant, and had more or less aborted his education before reaching secondary school. He said he bunked off to make more time to burgle houses. Sometimes I wondered if he exaggerated the audacity of his delinquency, for it seemed too extravagant for even the most precocious of juvenile offenders, and could sound almost boastful. But the suggestion of pride was, I suspected, deliberately misleading.

The crimes he described didn't sound cunning or calculated so much as compulsive. He stole things he neither wanted nor could conceivably hope to get away with, and something else he often said made me guess that if he was exaggerating, it was not to make himself look good but to confirm his fear that he was bad, and corroborate his sense of shame. This one particular anecdote came up time and time again.

Tony had been messing about on the street with a bunch of kids one night when a boy lobbed a rock at a neighbour's porch lamp. The glass shattered, everyone scarpered, and within half an hour the neighbour was knocking on the Wilkinsons' door. She was called Mrs Flood. That Tony could remember this detail when he was so terrible with names he called me D for the first year of our acquaintance tells you something about the significance of what happened next. 'Your son just smashed our lamp,' Mrs Flood told his mother. Tony was summoned to the door. 'Did you smash Mrs Flood's lamp?' He looked his mother in the face and without hesitation replied, 'Yes, I did.'

'Why did I say that?' he repeatedly puzzled. He wasn't trying to protect the guilty party, or misappropriate any status the act of random vandalism might confer. All of the other boys knew who had done it, so what was there to gain from a false confession?

The stories he told about adults in authority were almost unbearable to hear. As a boy he used to love cricket, until a coach made a false accusation against him, fully aware it was untrue. When challenged by Tony, the man took the ten-year-old off to a quiet corner and beat him up. On another occasion Tony was walking home from primary school with his sister through their leafy all-white suburb when a passing police car picked him up. Refusing to believe this could be where a black boy lived or had any business to be, the officers drove him to the inner-city Caribbean enclave of Chapeltown, where his parents had to come and collect him from the police station.

Tony was in his teens before he met another black person. On his first day at every new school he would be confronted by a familiar reception committee of kids keen to prove themselves. 'And what was I going to do? It was either them or me.' The inevitable reputation for violence was secured again, before the class register had even been taken.

Trans-racial adoption in the early Seventies was uncharted territory, and Tony never blamed his parents for struggling to understand the difficulties he found himself in. Racism was as bafflingly insensible to them as his behaviour. Nobody in their family had ever been in any sort of trouble before; they were out of their depth. But they were fiercely loyal, and that was what Tony remembered. Whenever Tony talked about his parents, he would revisit a memory of the night a middle-aged neighbour painted NIGGER on their gate. What lived with him was not the public humiliation, but the fury on his father's face in the morning when he saw it.

His father was not by nature combative. He might well have been the meekest man Tony ever knew – and it was a good job he was, Tony said, because he was not married to an easy woman. Tony's mother could insist the earth was flat – and by his account, her assertions were frequently no less outrageous – and his father would defer and placate and concur. But the couple's resolve to stand by their son was unassailable. When his father saw NIGGER daubed across the gate he turned pale, and stormed off to confront the neighbour.

Tony thought he had been only seven or eight when he saw a television documentary about street hustlers in Soho, who defrauded gullible punters hoping to buy sex or drugs. That, he decided, looked like the life for him. In early adolescence his court appearances grew more frequent, the periods of detention lengthened, and his hostility to authority hardened. The youth justice system was chaotic and arbitrary; sometimes he would be locked up in secure homes alongside children whose only crime had been to lose both their parents, and he was always particularly indignant on their behalf. If the authorities had imagined he would consider his own punishment legitimate, they were disappointed.

The only good to come of it was the loyalty his parents were called upon to prove, over and over again. If Tony was testing them, they did not fail. Had they given up on their son, I'm not sure that he would ever have been able to love, and might well have become dangerous enough to be capable of anything. As it was, he learned a concept of love that had little to do with intimacy, of which he had no experience, and everything to do with loyalty. But the boy his parents brought home from each incarceration had grown more unreachable, and at fifteen Tony ran away to London to realise his childhood ambition.

He was always rather nostalgic about his years as a hustler. Soho's seamy warren of alleyways became his teenage playground, and there was a certain daring glamour in his tales of touring the clip joints and late-night illegal drinking dens, promising fictional pornographic beauties to gullible tourists and passing off bags of tea leaves for cannabis, before disappearing into the shadows with pockets crammed full of cash. I said he must have been lonely and frightened, but if he was he had chosen to forget. Dodging the police was all part of the thrill, he said, and by his account an absorbing game of cat and mouse. His only unhappy memory was a surprising one. Having romanticised Caribbean culture for years back in Leeds, he had arrived in London with an Afro flat top and the carefully styled look of a Jamaican rude boy. The first actual black men he met were a shocking disappointment. 'I couldn't believe it,' he said. 'They just hung around the bookies all week, waiting for their giro. Then they'd get pissed and beat up their missus.'

By seventeen Tony had established himself as a highly proficient hustler, and was going out with a prostitute who worked for a gang of Jamaican pimps. After he helped her to escape their control, they broke into his south London squat at dawn and beat him with iron bars, before carting his girlfriend off to resume her services. Tony got hold of a gun, tracked them down and shot several of them. Nobody died, and he went on the run, until a little over a year later the police found him. He was still in his teens when he stood trial at the Old Bailey and was sentenced to fourteen years.

There was no glamour in his account of prison. Even though the sentence was reduced on appeal to seven years, he still served nearly five, much of it in segregation on account of violent non-compliance with the regime. Pragmatic self-interest was not a strategy with which Tony was psychologically familiar. He would have rather died – literally – than surrender to the authority of prison staff he considered more morally disreputable than most of the inmates, and his back never recovered from the beatings they inflicted. Resistance was a matter of principle. It even extended as far as temporarily turning vegan, simply in order to be a nuisance.

Two weeks after his release he met a young blonde Californian woman on a grand tour of Europe, who invited him to join her. They went travelling, moved to Los Angeles, and married a few years later at a $50 wedding chapel in Las Vegas.

According to Tony, the marriage was essentially expedient and transactional. He became a violent gangster who made a lot of money out of drugs, gunrunning, protection and so forth. She looked good, and liked spending it. It was a stormy relationship. Tony had a large stock of spectacular marital row anecdotes, which had the slightly worn air of many previous outings, and he often said that he should sue the Beach Boys for misleading him about the nature of California girls. Sometimes he claimed his wife had sprung the wedding on him in Vegas while he was drunk; at others he said they only married for immigration purposes. But when they had tried splitting up, he went to pieces. Tony was immensely proud of the fact his parents had both been virgins on their wedding day and remained together until his father's death some years ago, and it was clear that for all his well-trodden grumbles he maintained a powerful if sentimental attachment to the idea of marriage. He was often out with his daughter, but we very seldom saw his wife – I'd never once seen them together – and I think he liked it when people were surprised to discover he had been married for sixteen years.

As he grew more relaxed, I began to see that Tony enjoyed the idea of being an anomaly. 'You should write a book about me!' he was forever exclaiming. 'Seriously, you should. My life would make a wicked book.' It was certainly unconventional, I agreed. There had to be a market for a gangster memoir, he persisted; his own bookshelf proved it. At least half the titles on it were bestselling examples of the genre – 'And mine would be way better than any of them. Come on, D. You know you're going to write it one day.' I used to laugh and roll my eyes. Tony's narrative approach to his criminal adventures was so wildly erratic that I could never be sure what to believe, and didn't fancy my chances of taming the tangle into anything that might resemble a verifiable story. Besides, I told him, everyone always thinks their life would make a fascinating book.

In the early Nineties Tony and his wife moved back to London, and bought a flat on Ainsworth Road. Following the birth of their daughter in 1994, Tony wound up the more ostentatiously lawless aspects of his criminal lifestyle, and confined his business concerns to the discreet whole-sale trade of cocaine. For a year he attended church, to get his daughter into the local Church of England primary school, and despite neither believing in God nor having always been to bed the night before, he enjoyed his Sunday mornings with the matrons of the community. I imagine they were rather bowled over by him.

Most people were. Tony made all sorts of friends on Ainsworth Road – West Indian grandmothers, a gay neighbour dying of Aids, the publisher who lived next door to us – and at weekends would round up whoever he could find to go off touring festivals in his old VW camper van. When his daughter started school, and would need to explain how her father made a living, he opened an organic wholefood store, followed later by the property development company. As he saw it, he had practically gone legit.

At times I got the impression he genuinely believed he had. The tendency to mistake one's own deceptions for the truth is an occupational hazard in his line of work, and indeed may well be a prerequisite for success. Tony could work himself into such a fever of blameless umbrage, he would quite forget he was actually guilty as charged. I saw this for myself once or twice, when he arrived in a great froth of indignation after being stopped by the police on his way. He drove a large white 5-series BMW – not especially flash, for it was several years old, but ferociously high-powered – and Tony liked to put his foot down. He had been driving for ten years, was never without a spliff at the wheel, and had a relaxed attitude to drink-driving laws. What he did not have, however, was a driving licence. How he kept getting away with it – and he always did – was a mystery, but even more baffling was his outrage at the audacity of the police for pulling him over.

There was more to it than merely believing his own lies. At the heart of the confusion, I began to see, lay a deep ambivalence about his criminal career. It is no small achievement to break the law for so long without getting caught, and part of Tony was unapologetically proud of outwitting a system disgraced in his eyes by racism. If the law's sole purpose was to crush and humiliate him, the only self-respecting response was to break it. But another part of him felt ill at ease with a career that had consigned him to the margins. He loved talking about his old organic shop, and the palpable relish with which he dished out business cards for his property company suggested he rather coveted the casual freedom of legitimacy. What he had really enjoyed in church, I guessed, was the unfamiliar balm of acceptability.

My own ambivalence about his criminal status was

similarly unresolved, but slightly different. I had no moral problem with his job. How could I? I had happily enjoyed taking illegal drugs. Besides, if my own experience of the authorities had been anything like Tony's, my retaliation would probably have made him look like Uncle Tom. So his criminality was not the problem, in itself. What troubled me was whether my attraction to him was in spite or because of it. I very much hoped it was the former, and thus pleasing proof of my good liberal credentials. I worried that it could be the latter, and nothing but the cheap thrill of vicarious transgression.

The one thing of which Tony was unmistakably ashamed was his addiction to crack. I first learned of it from Paul, when he came home one night somewhat unnerved, after an evening with Tony and his friends. 'Bloody hell, Dec, they smoke *crack*.' I was shocked. Like most people who have taken recreational drugs, I had always drawn an important distinction between substances that enliven a night out and ones that ruin lives. Crack belonged firmly in the second category, and was no part of my world. The first time I saw anyone take it was the night Tony took out a small bag from his pocket, emptied the contents into a teaspoon, and began cooking it up over my Aga.

The appropriate response to someone smoking crack in one's kitchen is an etiquette challenge for which I was unprepared. I couldn't think what to say. I considered asking him to stop, but did not want to look prim, and the studied casualness with which Tony lit up made me suspect he was equally embarrassed. Unsure how to broach the subject, he had decided the best course would be to say nothing and act as if it were perfectly normal. I went along with the pretence for an hour or so, until curiosity got the better of me.

My questions quickly made him defensive. He first began using crack years ago, he said, but had quit when his daughter was born, and stayed clean for a long time. He blamed strains in his marriage, and the endless rows, for turning him back to it. Then he reeled off a long list of all the crucial differences between himself and the common or garden addict who steals his mother's pension to blow in a crack den.

For a start, he pointed out, he didn't smoke it in a pipe like a proper crackhead, but only in a cigarette – an altogether milder and more respectable delivery method. He only smoked at night time, and never until the day's business had been taken care of. He wasn't like those addicts who neglect their responsibilities. He did take it every night, but whenever he went abroad on holiday he would go a fortnight or more without it, so he couldn't really be an addict, could he? Besides, crack would only be a problem if he couldn't afford it. Given the nature of his profession, there was never any shortage of the raw materials, nor any need for him to associate with unsavoury types who sell rocks on the street. His daughter knew nothing about it, and his wife wanted for nothing. It wasn't as if he was raiding the family budget.

All of this was factually true, I soon came to see – but I did not believe that Tony really felt what mattered most about crack was its affordability. Nor did the idea that he was not technically an addict ring true. All of his justifications and strenuous protests sounded like the desperate sophistry of denial, and the person he was contriving to deceive was himself. I felt sorry for him. I had never met anyone who cared more about looking indomitable – invincible, even – or invested as much pride in the impression of strength. Crack addiction was a weakness he could not afford to acknowledge, even to himself.

Why I did not find it more off-putting was a puzzle. It was unedifying, certainly, and his transparent self-delusion only made it more disturbing. But there was a magnetism about Tony that eclipsed my reservations, and beneath all the bluster his longing for approval had a charm I found compelling. Then there was, too, the unavoidable fact of his beauty, mesmerising to the point of hypnotic. I noticed that I neglected to mention his visits to anyone. As Paul's return from Afghanistan drew near, I could no longer carry on pretending to myself that my feelings for Tony were entirely platonic.

Tony and I were struggling to sustain the pretence between ourselves. The increasingly charged atmosphere in my kitchen was never explicitly acknowledged, but a careless brush of a hand on a shoulder would be enough to make us breathless and freeze. One night, as he was about to leave he took my elbows in his hands and we stared at one another in silence. I thought he was about to kiss me. He dropped his hands, murmured 'You're not my woman,' turned and left. When a few nights later he suggested, very casually, that we should maybe go for lunch some time, we both understood what he was saying. 'Why not?' I agreed airily, as if nothing could be more mundanely innocent.

But once Paul was home I gave myself a talking-to. What had I been thinking? I must have been out of my mind. It was nothing but a silly schoolgirl crush, and had to be nipped in the bud before it got out of hand. I sent Tony a short text: 'I think we need to cool this now.' He texted back: 'Okay. If that's what you want.'

We scarcely saw each other for the next two months. When Tony invited us to Christmas drinks at his house, it felt perfectly safe to say yes. By then I had begun to doubt whether we had ever been in any real danger of allowing mild flirtation to escalate into something more significant. Probably not, I decided. Even if we had, the danger had now passed.

I have often wondered if that would have been the end of the matter, had it not been for three separate events in the following days. The evening after Tony's Christmas party I was shopping in Hackney when he texted me to say he was in a local bar, and did I fancy popping in for a drink? I found him in dejected spirits. There had been another nuclear-grade argument with his wife; he could not take any more, they had agreed to separate. The house was to be sold, and that summer she would be moving to Spain with their daughter. Their marriage was over. The following morning Paul and I drove down to my father's house in Wiltshire, where we endured one of those relationship-endingly horrific Christmases with which divorce lawyers in January are so famously familiar. And on Boxing Day the tsunami hit Southeast Asia.

Paul and I were barely speaking when he left for the airport to fly to Indonesia. He would be gone for at least a month, and even telephone contact looked unlikely, for the tsunami had wiped out most mobile-phone reception. It was hard to say which of us was more relieved to see the back of the other. Christmas had tipped a precariously unhappy marriage over the edge into free-fall crisis, and we both knew it.

I waited a few days before calling Tony. I think I was pretending not to know what was about to happen, as if ignorance could somehow absolve me of responsibility. It was late afternoon on his fortieth birthday when I sat in a window at the top of the house and dialled his number. He answered at the first ring. I took a deep breath. 'About that lunch. I've changed my mind.'

3

We met in a pub on the edge of Victoria Park, a five-minute walk from Ainsworth Road. I told myself it was only lunch, but averted my gaze from passers-by on the way, burning with nerves. Tony was standing at the bar when I arrived. The impulse to touch him took my breath away. The pub was practically empty, and in the hush I thought our hellos sounded artificially tinny.

We didn't eat. I don't remember either of us even suggesting it. We sat at a table in the corner and talked, knees and elbows brushing together. Nothing significant was said. It was a bitter January day, and by mid-afternoon the light was already failing when Tony suggested a stroll across the park. He was wearing a beige quilted coat, and as the wind whipped up he drew me into its warmth and wrapped his arm around me. The path was ankle-deep in dry leaves, and scrunched as we walked in silence. When we reached the trees on the far side near the canal, he lowered his head and kissed me.

The first kiss had been the central preoccupation of almost every magazine and novel I read when I was young, and a ceaseless topic for discussion among my friends. The discrepancy between thrilling accounts of fireworks and euphoria, and my personal experience in the clammy arms of boys half my height, was disappointing. But when Tony kissed me in the park, I thought I might actually faint. The intensity of joy was unlike anything I had ever known; I was weightless, delirious. We kissed again before he got in his car, and I floated home in a daze. I lay on the sofa and stared at the ceiling for six hours.

He phoned shortly after ten that night. We had never talked about our feelings for each other, but his voice was suddenly urgent. 'Look,' he said. 'I don't care how this sounds, and I don't know what it means for us. But Decca, I love you. That's all I've got to say.' I was stunned. He couldn't possibly mean it. We barely knew each other. 'I love you too,' I said.

Did I? I couldn't. It was preposterous, insane. Wasn't it? When I heard myself say the words again, they didn't feel like a lie. He said he had to go and see someone in north London, and would I like to come? He picked me up at the bottom of the road. 50 Cent was playing in the car, and as I stepped in a terrible fear seized me. If I could see myself now, would this look like nothing but an adolescent gangsta fantasy? Should I be embarrassed? But as he reached across and kissed me, I didn't care. I was lost.

All of Tony's caution had melted away. He held my hand as we drove, and his friend in Tottenham must have been startled to open his door to a pair of giggling sweethearts. While they talked in the kitchen I buried my face in the coat of his gigantic dog, until Tony led me out onto the balcony and his friend pretended not to notice while we kissed. When Tony dropped me home I lay awake until dawn, replaying the day in my head, smiling into the pillow.

What did I think we were doing? I had no idea. As I couldn't see the question leading anywhere particularly promising, I decided to stop asking. The truth was, I wasn't really thinking at all. I was already beyond reason, deranged by a chemical longing to be back in Tony's arms.

If I managed to do any work that month, I do not remember. Every day we would find somewhere to meet – in Tony's car by the canal, a dingy pub on Bethnal Green Road, his friend's flat in Hackney – and each assignation grew more unmanageably intense. We met in an ill-advisably chichi wine bar one night, and were quickly asked to leave; the manager said our kissing was making the other customers uncomfortable. We fell out of the door, laughing into the night, semi-hysterical with mortification. Neither of us was surprised; the sexual tension was making us uncomfortable too. Often Tony would be pouring with sweat by the time we parted, and I would walk home shaking.

For as long as we were only kissing, I told myself we

still had a choice. We could still pull back from the brink of what looked, in my clearer-headed moments, like incontrovertible lunacy. When I was away from Tony and could think straight, whatever it was that we shared began to seem ludicrously flimsy. Only a fool could expect it to bear the weight of anything as momentous as a decision to be together. He and I were so farcically incompatible in every way, I wondered whether the person each of us was falling for was nothing more than a fantasy of physical infatuation, and existed only in the confines of the other's fevered mind. At least once a day I resolved to end it. The resolve would last until the next time I saw him.

Before long our meetings assumed a familiar pattern. We would both agree that this had to stop at once. After all, I would point out, he was married. He would remind me that they had decided to separate. It was my understanding, I would say, that married men were notorious for saying that sort of thing. Exasperated by my scepticism, he would get huffy and point out that I was a married woman. 'I can't see that remaining the case for much longer,' I would say. He would protest: 'But you've got a lovely husband, and a great life. Look at me, Dec – I'm a criminal. No one in your world would want you to be with me. If you were my daughter, I wouldn't want you to be with me either.' It was, we would agree, hopeless. Then we would kiss until our lips burned and people began to stare. Before parting we would tell each other this was absolutely the last time we would meet. The promise didn't always last long enough for us to get home. After a particularly anguished farewell I hadn't got out of second gear before my phone pinged. 'HC?' the text read. I turned the car around and was back with him in a bar called Hackney Central in under five minutes.

When Tony's wife and daughter went away on holiday for a week, our meetings grew longer but no less agitated or inconclusive. The night before their return we spent hours on the phone, revisiting the impossibility of the situation. Surely this had to be the end, once and for all. I hung up, desolate but decisive. A minute later the phone rang again. 'Tone, we've agreed this can't go on,' I told him sternly. 'Dec,' he said, in a voice I scarcely recognised. 'My mum's died. My brother just called. She's dead. I need to see you.'

I got dressed and drove to his house. Since that day in the park both our homes had been out of bounds; the injunction was unspoken but did not need to be stated, and as I knocked on his door it felt like trespass. All fastidiousness was forgotten when he opened it. Tony looked shell-shocked, his eyes vacant and black. His mother hadn't been well, but no one had dreamt her condition was critical. I rocked him in my arms on the living-room sofa until dawn broke and his wife and daughter would soon be arriving home. For once we didn't bother to pretend we were saying goodbye.

On the day Paul came home Tony was in Leeds with his family, taking care of funeral arrangements. I hoped the 200 miles between us might create some space to accommodate the sudden intrusion of reality – spouses, families, bereavement – and wondered if Paul's reappearance would bring me to my senses. When he arrived there was a stiff, mechanical quality to our embrace, and a lifelessness in our conversation more deathly than any I could recall. Every attempt at a genuine exchange seemed to run out of steam, tailing off into claustrophobic silence. We were like distant colleagues in a lift.

I had organised a welcome-home dinner the following night. My cousin Ewan would be joining us. Halfway through cooking I realised we needed sour cream, so jumped in the car to pop to the supermarket. On my way I called Tony. He was back from Leeds, and in a café around the corner. We met in a side street behind the supermarket. I climbed into his car and clung to him like to a life raft. I can't have been in his car for more than three minutes, but long enough to know that I was about to go home for the last time. Whatever happened next, it couldn't be this.

The dinner passed in a charade of distraction, while my words and my thoughts parted company. 'Pass the pepper, please.' Am I seriously going to leave Paul for Tony? Of course not. 'Tell us about your new job, Ewan.' Then am I leaving Paul because of Tony? Well yes, obviously. But not because I think Tony and I have a future. We would be miserable together. If I couldn't make a life with Paul work, I'm hardly going to manage it with a crack-smoking drug dealer. 'What was the press pack like in Indonesia? . . . Who was out there with you?' I have to leave, because I cannot be sneaking about having illicit trysts behind supermarkets – it is shameful, this can't be who I am. If I cannot keep away from Tony now that Paul is back, the only option with any shred of integrity is to leave. What happens after that is irrelevant, so there's no point even trying to work out a plan. 'There's coffee if anyone would like some,' I say.

Was it even integrity? I wasn't sure. It might be staggering naïvety. All I knew was that for all of my life until Tony, I had been immune to infidelity. This was nothing to boast about, for it had nothing to do with virtue. It was simply that I had never been tempted to stray. Even with the most comedic of comedy boyfriends, it didn't occur to me to be anything other than faithful, because I never looked at anyone else. Now I could not look my own husband in the eye. A longing to go to bed with Tony was no reason to think I could spend my life with him, but enough to tell me I could not be with Paul.

I scrutinised my own logic anxiously. Was I being ridiculous? Other people happily spend half their married lives fancying someone else. They're not unworldly enough to mistake common temptation for marital curtains. If only I was French. I still loved my husband, even if I couldn't stand to be with him; the horror of deceit made me nauseous. Or was I just pretending to be appalled, in order to dress up cheap betrayal in bogus honour?

After Paul went to bed I sat up late, gazing down on Ainsworth Road from a top-floor window. I thought about our wedding day, and about our families, and our friends. I pictured an imaginary grenade in my hand. Was I really about to pull the pin and lob it into this life we had built together? I wondered what would be left after the explosion.

My bag was packed before Paul awoke. 'I'm leaving,' I told him. The air was flat, deadened by defeat. 'Okay,' he said quietly. 'I'll be at Tom and Charlotte's,' I said. 'Okay,' he said. I drove to our old friends in Kentish Town, wondering what they would say, and what I had done. They were taken aback. They put me in the spare room, and I thought I would stay for perhaps a week or two while I worked out what to do.

Two days later Tony called and asked to meet me in Hackney. As he got out of his car, I saw a large black canvas holdall in one hand. He held it up, in the manner of a chancellor on budget day. 'I've left,' he announced breathlessly. What was he talking about? It took me a moment to register what he meant. 'I've left. I want to be with you. You're my girl now.'

And that was how Tony and I became the most implausible couple I have ever known.

If you have nowhere to live in London, need to find somewhere fast, and don't own the most rudimentary household items – vacuum cleaner, ironing board, kettle – where do you go? Tony was the sort of person who always knew someone to call. He had a friend who owned a lettings agency – 'Bit dodgy,' Tony grinned, 'but he owes me a favour' – so after a quick call we made our way to the office.

Should Channel 4 ever want to make a docusoap about the East End property market, I could show them just the place to film. When we first walked in I half wondered whether cameras weren't already installed, for every detail had been so finely observed – the directional haircuts and ski tans, the rhyming slang and restless testosterone – the room looked more like a reality TV set than real life. All the young men seemed to know Tony, and were on their feet in a flash. As I watched them fizz and buzz around him, competing for his wisecracks ('Think you've got enough gel in that hairdo, mate?', 'Call that a watch?'), I saw the extraordinary effect he had on other men. By my terms, Tony's social technique was borderline rude. Men found it mysteriously flattering, and compelling.

What we needed, Tony explained to the boss, was a short-term lease on a fully furnished flat equipped with everything right down to teaspoons. 'Well that's Canary Wharf, Tone, innit?' I thought he had to be joking. I wasn't living there. In an improbability contest, moving to Canary Wharf would beat leaving my husband for a drug dealer hands down.

Canary Wharf is a brutally modern development of shiny skyscrapers in what used to be London's old East End docklands. Only a few miles south of Hackney, it feels more like Tokyo. Early each morning, driverless trains deliver young professionals in suits to their desks in the glittering high-rise concrete forest where they sit at screens all day making multinationals richer until it's time to eat sushi in air-conditioned branches of international restaurant chains, or work out in corporate gyms. It looks like a child's drawing of capitalist alienation – only, of course, there are few children there to draw it. There aren't really any old people either, nor any trees, or greenery, or clutter. It was my idea of perfect hell. Now it was my new home. By teatime we had rented the sort of executive apartment designed for IT executives from Shanghai who like concrete and glass; it made me feel as if we had gone into internal exile.

Panic mounted when we unpacked our respective bags. Tony kept returning from his car with more armfuls of clothes – designer jeans, endless boots, pair after pair of identical trainers – and wrestled to cram them into his half of the wardrobe. When I had hung all of mine up, they occupied less than nine inches of rail. The comically lop-sided spectacle made us both laugh, but as a metaphor for what we had embarked on it felt ominous. I was moving in with someone so fantastically unlike me, even our wardrobe looked like a joke. The recklessness of sudden domestic intimacy with a man I had only just slept with hit me again next morning, when we stood side by side in the bathroom brushing our teeth. I could see our faces in the mirror, but the reflection felt unreal, as if an imposter had kidnapped my identity.

After a week I went home and told Paul I was seeing Tony. To keep him in the dark was unconscionable; he had a right to know. But when it came to full disclosure, the cohabitation detail was beyond me, and I told Paul I was living alone. I told myself it was a kindness – that the whole truth would be gratuitously cruel – but suspected altruism might be a convenient disguise for the real reason.

Paul had absorbed my announcement about Tony with the terse dignity I would have predicted. I was afraid the news that we were living together might make him laugh. The new domestic arrangement was still startling to me, and my own faith in its wisdom too shaky to withstand incredulity.

Living in Canary Wharf quickly proved every bit as awful as expected. Tony's cannabis smoke wafting down magnolia corridors freaked our new neighbours out a lot. His after-dinner progression onto crack troubled me similarly. Even watching television together presented a challenge. Tony liked action superhero movies featuring multiple body counts, whereas I favoured programmes in which nobody gets blown up. By a stroke of luck we soon stumbled upon *The Sopranos*, a discovery without which I would go as far as to say we almost certainly would not have lasted more than a month. But bit by bit we began to find our feet, and found scraps of territory beyond our sofa that could accommodate our incongruity.

At first it was long car journeys. Road trips can often curate conversational intimacy, but in our case the charm was not what was said so much as how Tony drove. Although fast, he was never aggressive at the wheel, and nothing ever fazed him; unlike me he was quite immune to road rage, and I don't think I once saw him sound his horn or flash his lights. I found the calmness of his gallantry at the wheel inexpressibly soothing, and could sit beside him for hours, lost in the childlike sensation of security.

Football matches and boxing fights also seemed to work.

In any theatre of masculinity Tony would come alive, and I liked to watch him magnetise other men. Their eagerness to defer was intriguing. Men always claim to be oblivious to masculine beauty, which is obviously a lie, because in my experience the presence of a good-looking man usually generates a wary unease. Given the competitive subtext of most male interactions, this is not terribly surprising. But Tony's beauty had the opposite effect, and seemed to excite men. They liked to cluster around him, as if proximity could confer vicarious glamour, and were forever wanting to give him something. It happened everywhere we went. Shopkeepers, market traders and restaurant waiters, unsolicited and for no discernible motive, would give him something for free. Tony was always pleased, but too used to it to be surprised.

In Tony's presence men tended to lose interest in women, and on his arm I became acquainted with the novel status of a social passenger. In previous relationships I had been the dominant social force – the loud, bossy one – and it was surprisingly relaxing to be released from the role. Relieved of responsibility for making it work, a night out in Tony's world often felt like a social anthropology field trip.

It was only in the company of my friends that the roles reversed, and all of Tony's confidence melted away. Worried about what they would think of him, he assumed the worst, and paranoia could put him in danger of fulfilling the prophecy. In dismay I would watch him grow sullen and withdrawn, or boorish and overbearing, or edgy

Decca Aitkenhead

and distracted. I would overcompensate by laughing too much, shrill with insincerity, while my bewildered friends made heroic efforts to act as if we were a perfectly normal couple.

In Tony's circle my middle-class manners were neither normal, nor massively successful. Perhaps a little over half his friends were white, the rest black, and a lot were or had been criminals, though far from all. But they were all men, and observed a social code to which my conversational approach was ill-suited. In my world, curiosity is the key to social success; if you want to ingratiate or flatter or show respect, you ask questions. So I did. In Tony's world, to question someone you've just met – or for that matter, anyone – was a calamitous faux pas guaranteed to provoke offence and suspicion. Several friends quietly suggested to him that I was an undercover police officer. His news that I was in fact a journalist was not found reassuring.

I can recall only one occasion when a friend of Tony's asked me questions about myself. We had already met lots of times, and I liked him enormously; he was a drug dealer from Hackney in his mid-twenties, white and skinny, with a Dickensian pallor to suggest minimal exposure to daylight. Always late for everything, he would burst in with a great flurry of excuses about far-fetched misfortunes, a surprising number of which would turn out to be true. Everyone had an anecdote about his propensity to land himself in trouble, and perhaps it was his status as the loveable clown that licensed him to break the code and ask me questions. He was curious about my job: how did an article get commissioned, was I allowed to write whatever I wanted, who made up the headline? I was amazed, and rather touched. The conversation lasted only a few minutes before he clamped a hand over his mouth. 'God, mate, sorry. What must you be thinking? Dunno what happened there. Talk about embarrassing. I'm really sorry. You must think I'm coming on like Old Bill.'

If Tony and I came from different social worlds, we also occupied separate time zones. I would generally get up around 8 a.m., and work at my desk in the spare room until he woke up at around four in the afternoon. His day would start with coffee, a spliff, Sky News, and a quick-fire burst of phone calls. As he tended to be quite grumpy when first awake, he had worked out that this was the ideal time to phone everyone who owed him money. His threats were seldom particularly inventive or colourful; they didn't need to be. The sound of his growl through the wall was menacing enough to make me jump, and quite hard to reconcile with the sleepy smile and gentle kiss he would pad through in his slippers to deliver to me at my desk.

Once he was up and about, there was usually business to attend to. This consisted largely of 'meets'. He had a personal mobile, and a work one whose number would be regularly changed, but nothing of any significance could be discussed over the phone, so he would head off to meet associates in car parks or pubs, or they would show up at our flat and disappear into the bedroom with Tony. Before long the cast of faces became familiar, and we would ex-change pleasantries and drink tea before they retired to talk business, for all the world as if I were a housewife married to a reputable entrepreneur.

The truth was that Tony's work was quite boring. When I told friends about it, they pictured Hollywood gangsta high drama – car chases, concealed weapons, death threats – and were disappointed to learn that it was mostly just phone calls and meets. He employed a City accountant whose client base consisted exclusively of criminals, and who specialised in producing false accounts convincing enough to satisfy the Inland Revenue. The cocaine was stored in a safe house two boroughs away, but even that turned out to be less exciting than it sounded; it was just a bloke's flat on a council estate. Occasionally there would be a dispute with a supplier about the purity of a consignment, and Tony would come home in a bad mood. But he was always reluctant to go into details about his work, on the sensible principle that should the police ever show up, if I knew nothing I would be unable to tell them anything. As information could only compromise me, I was happy with this arrangement, although oddly enough I never worried about the police. Tony's business operation seemed too mundane to be risky, and the possibility that he might get caught did not enter my mind.

As far as I could see, there was only one major flaw in his business model, but it destabilised the entire drug-dealing economy; this was credit. Every purchase Tony made was on tick, and his supplier would be paid only once Tony had sold the consignment on – but Tony's clients could only pay him when they had in turn sold it on and been repaid, so the economy consisted of a long daisy chain of loans. Given the precarious nature of the business, and the character of some of the parties involved, the chain frequently broke down. Without recourse to legitimate means of recovering money owed, the threat of violence was embedded in the terms and conditions of business. To achieve the desired leverage, it needed to be credible.

Tony was very open about his relationship with violence. It used to be his favourite part of the job, he said, and recreational violence had been tremendous fun too. He had no interest in gratuitous non-consensual violence, and only contempt for nutters who pick fights in pubs with innocent or defenceless strangers. Any man who hit a woman or child was beyond the pale. The rules of engagement, as he saw it, were straightforward. If violence wasn't justified as a necessary business tool, it could be legitimately deployed only if the other party provoked it, or was equally enthusiastic about having a fight. The latter scenario was his favourite, and explained his fondness for football hooliganism. He had travelled all over the world supporting England, but sometimes never even made it to the game, for the football was only a sideshow, and the main attraction the rival hooligans also there only for the fighting.

I tried to get him to explain the pleasure of violence, but to Tony it was so self-evident that my questions made little sense. It would be like explaining why sex or chocolate or dancing were enjoyable; they just were. But lately, he did say, he had begun to notice something strange. The appeal seemed to be fading. He still enjoyed the sense of power an impression of threat conferred, but when required to service the reputation, he was finding it curiously unrewarding.

I witnessed violence only once for myself. We were driving through Hackney when he spotted someone who owed him money. He pulled over calmly, got out and went to talk to him. I watched in the rear-view mirror as they exchanged a few words. There was no shouting, no altercation, no drama. Then Tony head-butted him. The man crumpled onto the pavement in a heap. Tony got back in the car and equally calmly drove on. If I hadn't been looking, I don't think I would have been able to believe he had just knocked a man out.

Once the day's business was concluded he would usually take me to his gym, where he would run and I would swim, after which we would have a steam and sauna and go for supper. Then he would open a beer and smoke crack. Having never been around anyone else who smoked it, I had nothing with which to compare the drug's effect on Tony, but it was certainly less dramatic than government health warnings had led me to believe. Crack did not transform him into a ravening paranoid lunatic; it just made him garrulous and rather repetitive. Around one I would usually go to bed, and he would sit up smoking and watching Sky News until dawn. I complained that it meant he was asleep all day, but my sense that this was not normal surprised him. I was always busy at my desk, he would reason, and no one else in his line of work would be awake either, so where would be the point in getting up any earlier?

My memories of those months in Canary Wharf have

a dreamlike, fantasy quality which did not only materialise retrospectively. In real time there was always at least one moment every day when I surveyed the situation and thought I must have lost my mind. How had I landed in this bizarre new life that clearly did not belong to me? I understood that my marriage was over; that I had had to leave, but I hadn't meant to swap it overnight for setting up home with Tony. He couldn't understand what I was doing with him either. He thought I might be involved in an elaborate journalistic experiment, in which I had sacrificed my marriage to go undercover and write an exposé of east London gangsters – because why else was I there? I couldn't answer the question, because I didn't know.

All I knew was how I felt when I was with him. I loved the way he smelt, and the way he moved. I loved the un-complicated intensity of his loyalty. Having fallen in love, he saw no cause to reconsider or re-evaluate his feelings; I was his girl, he loved me, and nothing else mattered more to him than that. That we were profoundly differ-ent did not trouble him. He was shamelessly proud of my work, read everything I wrote, and would often make his friends read it too. 'Look at this! Dec wrote this!' he would exclaim, shoving the latest article under a startled visitor's nose. News and current affairs fascinated him. Emphatically Labour, his relationship with politics was more visceral than intellectual, but his instincts often proved unexpectedly accurate. Gordon Brown was going to be a disastrous prime minister, he repeatedly assured me. I told him he didn't know what he was talking about.

Although we agreed about a lot of other political beliefs, in the early days I found his opinions almost laughably random. In the absence of an educated ideological framework, they struck me as arbitrary and baseless. Gradually I began to see that what I liked to think of as my own ideological framework was really just a mental apparatus of prejudice, and that while Tony's way of looking at the world could be maddeningly unpredictable, it was also liberating. He was genuinely without prejudice.

He was also the least self-pitying person I have ever met. As he saw it, he was lucky to be alive. His mother could have aborted him, he might easily have been abandoned to the care system, and his adoptive parents would have been well within their rights to reject him. Having survived homelessness, prison and life-threatening violence he felt equal to anything, and his self-belief made the world glitter with possibility. Indomitable optimism inclined him to see the best in others, and I loved the generosity of his respect for young men. 'Hello big guy,' he would greet a gawky teenager, making the boy swell and glow. Even when people let him down he could seldom stay angry for long, for he was incapable of bearing a grudge, and I found his capacity for forgiveness rather humbling.

Above all, I loved the way Tony confounded expectations, for he was nothing like the person a stranger would guess from reading a bullet-point profile. Although a criminal, he was trustworthy and surprisingly guileless. His conversational style was often combative and prone to bluster, but out of nowhere he could admit to feeling frightened or unsure, and the flashes of vulnerability would always disarm me. They were never manipulative, for he was not emotionally calculating. He was not calculating at all. It was he, in fact, who pointed out to me that it was easy to tell when he told a lie because he couldn't help smiling.

In addition to the extensive wardrobe Tony had a particular fondness for manicures; he liked to have his nails not merely filed and buffed but glossed with a layer of lacquer, and he was never without a pot of Nivea in his car. Yet he was oblivious to the impact of his own beauty, and delighted by my careless indifference to make-up or grooming. When the occasion required, he could also be surprisingly willing to make a fool of himself.

We were in a south London bar late one night when I first witnessed this. We arrived late, after hours; one of his friends had invited us to join the lock-in, and as we approached the front door Tony mumbled a half-warning that it was a 'villains' sort of gaff'. Upstairs we found a dimly lit room full of edgy-looking men. The tension suggested cocaine had featured heavily in the evening's refreshments, and whatever chatty festivity this might have facilitated earlier had hardened into moody silence. Among the clientele were several men in the unmistakable stages of advanced paranoia. At a table in one corner sat a group of Australian tourists, cheerfully drunk and quite oblivious to the imminent danger. How they had found themselves in such a venue was a mystery, but it was perfectly clear that they were about to be beaten up. After greeting his friends and ordering drinks, Tony strolled over to the karaoke machine in another corner, set it up quietly, launched into an aggressive hardcore breakbeat intro – and sang Elton John's 'Your Song'. The room burst out laughing. Within minutes others were up on their feet singing Robbie Williams, and while no one was looking Tony quietly ushered the Australians out to safety.

We didn't often encounter karaoke, but whenever we did Tony was perplexed by my implacable refusal to take part. 'Come on Dec, it's only a laugh,' he would urge. 'What's your problem?' But to impersonate a performer in public requires a degree of disinhibition that was simply beyond me. Over time my intransigence came to irritate him, and I had a disagreeable suspicion that it reflected badly on me. An inability to suspend critical faculties and surrender to mindless joy is nothing to be proud of, and I envied Tony's unselfconscious indifference to his own dignity. One night in the Groucho club, a private members' club for media and arts professionals, Tony took to the floor to perform a vigorous duet of Meat Loaf's 'Bat out of Hell' with a chinless middle-aged Tory MP who, at the time of writing, is now the secretary of state for culture.

If misogyny and homophobia are traditional gangster qualities, Tony was unsuited to the role. He adored Barry Manilow, could listen to Christina Aguilera's 'Beautiful' on a loop, had a deep hippy streak, and loved camping, cooking and cleaning. His enthusiasms were boundless, unmediated by any concession to the protocol of contemporary cool. Tony's all-time favourite television programme was a weekly BBC report on rural affairs called *Countryfile*.

That our relationship nevertheless looked untenable was as obvious to me as it was to everyone else except Tony. Once he relaxed among my friends they came to like him tremendously, but could not see us having a future together. 'He's lovely,' I remember one venturing delicately after meeting him for lunch. 'But Decca, I'm not sure he's the man for you.' My family was even less willing to suspend disbelief.

The closest brother in age and geography was Tom, a record producer who lived in Hackney. In temperament, also, Tom and I were closest; he was one of my best friends. Unfortunately, however, in the course of my marriage he had become Paul's best friend too, and this created an initial conflict of interest in his relationship with Tony. My eldest brother was Ben, a banker in Manhattan who was married with three children and whom I saw at most once a year. Ben and I were too distant to share long-distance-call confidences, and most of what he heard about Tony would be filtered through the family grapevine.

What I had not yet appreciated was that the chief source of grapevine information was Paul, who remained close to my family, and was understandably disinclined to portray Tony in a flattering light.

The middle brother was Matt, who lived in Gloucestershire and owned a building company. Laddish and mischievous, I imagined he might get along with Tony – and the first few times they met I thought he did. My misreading of the situation only became clear at a family gathering so shatteringly ugly that my memory has deleted most of the details.

I was aware that my father found my separation from Paul incomprehensible and heartbreaking, so did not consider bringing Tony when we gathered at his house in Wiltshire. What was supposed to be some sort of family celebration began to fall apart as the depth of hostility towards me became horribly apparent. Whispered conversations would be abruptly aborted as I entered a room, eyes were averted, and when the tension became unbearable I announced I was leaving. What followed was a horrifying travesty of an intervention. One by one my extended family informed me that my behaviour was disgraceful. How could I treat Paul so abominably? What was I doing with a crack addict? 'You fucked him in your and Paul's house!' Matt screamed at me. 'What?' I yelled back. 'That's what Paul said!' 'Well he's hardly a reliable witness, under the circumstances, is he? Why the fuck would you believe that?' 'Because he's not a fucking criminal like your new boyfriend!' I stormed out, drove back to London, and with the exception of Tom, who apologised within days, did not speak to any of them again for a very long time.

A few friends who did not know my family assumed, when they learned of the estrangement, that Tony's race played a part in their disapproval. I was furious with my family, and so wounded by what had been said that I would have been ready to accuse them of almost anything, but the idea that racism had anything to do with it was ridiculous. The colour of Tony's skin was probably the only thing about him they didn't mind.

My judgement of wider prejudice levels was less reliable. Race felt so unimportant that when describing Tony I would sometimes forget to mention it, for in multicultural millennial Hackney I could not recognise the racism he had experienced as a youngster. I thought it belonged to another place and time altogether. My brother Ben had married a Nigerian American, and over the years his tales of Manhattan waiters' rudeness, watchful shop assistants, and apartment buildings where a mixed-race family was not welcome, had astonished me; nothing like that would ever happen in London. When I mentioned some of Ben's most eye-opening anecdotes to Tony, though, he found them unremarkable, and before long I began to see why. Tony liked to joke that we were Black and Decca – he had a terrible weakness for puns – but it wasn't always funny, and on his arm I was introduced to a degree of subtle racism of which I had till then been largely unaware.

By early summer, after several months of exile in Canary Wharf, we were desperate to move back to Hackney. I viewed a loft apartment, signed a lease, and paid the deposit. But after Tony collected the keys from the estate agency, the agent quickly phoned me. His new tone was surly and affronted. 'That man – he isn't going to be *living* there with you, is he?' Later that summer friends of mine got married in a lavish *OK!* magazine wedding, and Tony did not want to come. 'Dec I'll be the only black man there, I'll be out of place, I don't want to go.' I told him not to be daft. The groom was Derek Draper, a psycho-therapist and senior Labour party strategist; his bride, Kate Garraway, was a television presenter. How could Tony look out of place at a metropolitan media and politics wedding? In an Armani suit he looked like a model. When we arrived at the grand hotel on Piccadilly, I saw what he meant. Among the 300 or so faces I spotted one Asian woman, and the *OK!* photographers circulating among the guests kept asking Tony to move out of frame – they didn't want 'security staff' in the pictures.

As it turned out, the letting agent did not need to worry about Tony for long. A few weeks after we moved back to Hackney, he told me he had to move home to his wife and daughter. They were meant to be moving to Spain at the end of the summer, and as far as he could see nothing was being done to make it happen. The house had to be packed up and sold, belongings were to be divided, and unless he went home and took charge he was afraid none of it would get done. I was unsure what to make of his announcement. Part of me thought it sounded like a sensible precaution, another part was relieved at the prospect of some domestic space to catch breath and take stock, and part of me wondered if I had fallen for the oldest cliché in the book. Was I about to become the other woman, holed up in a mistress pad for Tony to visit and have fun with while resuming a married life he had no intention of ending? His wife and daughter hadn't any inkling of our relationship; they believed he had been staying with an old friend. Was he now lying to me too?

I half expected to end our relationship myself once he moved out anyway, for this surreal arrangement could not continue indefinitely. I was thirty-four years old, estranged from my family, and had a husband I still cared for deeply, who was living in our house among all our things, while I camped out in a loft with a man who smoked crack and was about to move home to his wife. Something had to give.

I didn't end it. We continued to see each other every day, and I sensed nothing to make me doubt Tony's intentions. On the face of it he would be easy to mistake for an extramarital womaniser, but in fact Tony's relationship with women was rather vulnerable and old-fashioned. Women made him nervous, he said, because with men he knew that if everything went horribly wrong, in the final resort there was always violence to fall back on. In the absence of that option he felt naked. He was much more at ease in the company of men. He was also easily embarrassed. Many of his friends were regular clients of strip clubs and prostitutes, but the sex industry made Tony cringe and blush, and once or twice he reappeared early from a night out because someone had called in a stripper, 'And Dec I had to get out of there, it was rank.'

In late August his wife and daughter left for Spain. The house was sold. Tony moved back in with me. It was the weekend Hurricane Katrina hit New Orleans, and we were glued to the television. As we stared at people stranded on rooftops, pleading for help, I considered my situation and realised that however unlikely it might look, I was fantastically lucky. I was living with a man I loved. What else could matter? The future would bring what it would bring. Whatever happened next, it would all work out fine.

A week later I discovered I was pregnant.

There was not a great deal to discuss. That I had to terminate the pregnancy was self-evident to us both, and the procedure was straightforward, for I was too early to require a hospital visit. A doctor gave me two pills, and that was that. But the simplicity of the decision was the issue, for a relationship in which a baby was literally thinkable was no longer one I could sustain. It wasn't that I was in any hurry to have children; I wasn't sure I would ever want them at all. But I could not be with a man whose lifestyle made the very idea unconscionably irresponsible.

We had a long, agonising discussion. The conclusion was that Tony would smoke crack only at weekends. It is a measure of how far I had drifted from reality that I thought this might be a workable solution. The following evening he did not come home from the gym until the early hours, or answer his phone. I was asleep by the time he got in. There was no point waiting up, because there was nothing to say.

I left the letter by his bedside before leaving in the morning. It said I loved him, but did not want to be with an addict. We were over. I caught a bus to Islington, sat in a coffee shop and cried, and went and spent a fortune on a coat, the most expensive item of clothing I had ever bought. I was at the till when my phone pinged with a text from Tony. 'I'm gone.'

4

To deny any trace of relief would be a lie. The end had always been coming, and inevitability offered some consolation of sorts while I tried to reframe the relationship in terms that might maximise the relief and mitigate the loss. The most successful strategy I found was to think of my romance with Tony as an embarrassing collision of clichés. I was the posh girl who fell for a bad boy. Secret assignations behind my husband's back had been a textbook case of seven-year itch. Running off with the neighbour was the laziest marital plotline of every cheap sitcom, and falling out with one's family over an unsuitable boyfriend the least original form of sub-adolescent rebellion. To hope that a crack addict could control his habit was so notoriously stupid, my naïvety made me cringe. Once

I put my mind to it, making my romance with Tony look like a mortifying lapse of judgement was easy. The hard part was making myself feel glad it was over.

I was inconsolable. London felt like a rainy seaside resort out of season; all the colour had faded into grey, and life looked drab and pointless. I spent a great deal of time in my pyjamas. On bonfire night I went to a fireworks display in Victoria Park. More than breathtakingly beautiful, it was imaginative and clever, and the vast crowd cooed and cheered in wonderment. Fuck you all, I glowered in the darkness. Fuck you for squealing on cue at a fucking Catherine wheel. Fuck your health-and-safety-approved fun in your fucking Cath Kidston wellies.

It was two weeks before Tony called. By then I had rehearsed the conversation a thousand different ways, but none of my imaginary scripts had prepared me for what he had to say.

The day he read my note and left, he had looked up the nearest Narcotics Anonymous group and attended his first meeting that evening. He found a local Cocaine Anonymous group too, and had been attending a meeting of one or other every day. Since I last saw him he had not touched crack. More incredibly still, he said he had felt no desire to. He was staying with an old friend who smoked crack most nights, but according to Tony the meetings had inoculated him against even the temptation to join in.

How was this possible? I could hardly believe my ears. But I knew Tony was not lying. As he described this mind-blowing new thrill of emotional honesty to me, he sounded euphoric. In the draughty church halls and community centres where recovering addicts gather, Tony had stumbled upon a context that released him from the guarded gangster code, and allowed him to connect with men in a register much more suited to who he really was. He couldn't get enough of it. His phone was full of new numbers, and in this new fraternity Tony was in his element. He loved the organised gallantry, the elaborate declarations of brotherly support, the ceaseless text messages checking up on each other.

I told him it was amazing – and it was. What I did not say, but did not doubt, was that it wouldn't last. How could it? For a start, most addicts relapse sooner or later, even when they follow the twelve-step programme to the letter. In Tony's case I could not see how it would work when he was disregarding the fellowship's insistence upon total abstinence. As he was continuing to smoke cannabis and drink, it could only be a matter of time before crack made a reappearance. On the other hand, to be less than encouraging while it lasted felt gratuitously unkind, and within days we were seeing each other again. After a month or so it seemed mad to make him keep living with a friend who smoked crack, so he moved back in with me. For many months after that I kept waiting for him to fall off the wagon, and after a while he did stop going to meetings. But he never touched crack again.

It was my first intimation of a quality in Tony that made him unlike anyone else I have ever known. Most of us talk all the time about how we are going to change, but good intentions seldom translate into action, and rarely last even when they do. When Tony put his mind to something, he was capable of almost anything.

The novelty of talking truthfully about his feelings began to open his eyes to all sorts of other possibilities. He enrolled at the local college and took courses in drug awareness and counselling. In the course of role-play workshops he made the revelatory discovery that he was an appalling listener, and began to notice that no one else in his circles listened to a word anyone said either. They were just waiting for their turn to talk. As he began to pay closer attention he realised that no one said anything interesting anyway. He was suddenly bored, and hungry for something more.

Why Tony had fallen in love with me was a question I used to puzzle over, and that was now becoming clearer. With the exception of the police, no one in his life had ever questioned him closely about himself, or listened carefully to his answers. 'You ask all these questions cos you're a journalist,' he used to say in the early days. 'No,' I would disagree, 'I became a journalist because I'm interested in people.' Tony was beginning to become interested in himself, and to re-examine his past for more complex clues than the account he had constructed out of crude headlines: Racism, Prison, Unhappy Marriage.

There was a conspicuous rigidity in his insistence that he felt nothing but gratitude for having been adopted which had often made me wonder, so I bought him a book about adoption called *The Primal Wound*. He read it in one sitting, transfixed. 'Dec, it's like reading my own diary.' The pain of rejection he had always tried to deny manifests itself, he read, in behaviours which adopted children and their parents often find bewildering, and explained his compulsion to steal and run away in terms he had never considered. The possibility that all parties involved in his adoption could be blameless, and yet still the adoption could have damaged him profoundly, was sensational. Tony found a therapist, and saw her every week for the rest of his life.

I talked him into sitting a driving test, and he passed. In the new year we moved to a flat in Kentish Town, and that spring I took him to Treasure Beach. Tony had never wanted to go to Jamaica, and told me so repeatedly. 'Bloody Yardies,' he would protest indignantly, 'they've caused me nothing but trouble. Why would I want to go to Jamaica?' I had a feeling he might change his mind, and within twenty-four hours of arriving he had fallen in love. He looked like he had lived there all his life. Treasure Beach Jamaicans tend to be golden brown rather than black, with broad features similar to Tony's, and in the first few days several villagers flagged our car down, mistaking him for a new local taxi driver.

That summer we threw a big house party in Kentish Town, and our respective friends began to get to know one another. My cat from Ainsworth Road came to live with us. We befriended the children who lived in the flat upstairs, a sweet-natured mixed-race boy and girl who trailed after Tony with puppy-dog eyes. Sometimes, as we fooled around with them in the garden, I could almost picture us having a family of our own.

Two problems remained seemingly insoluble. One was Tony's profession, which could just about be accommodated in our current lifestyle, but not reconciled in my mind with parenthood. The other was the hostility of his wife and daughter. I had no direct dealings with his wife, and could tell Tony preferred to keep the ugliest details of their rows to himself, but even his edited accounts were alarming. When his wife heard that he had stopped smoking crack, Tony said she had been happy for him. When she learned of our relationship, the realisation that he had quit for me was incendiary.

There were days when I wondered if it was hopelessly unrealistic to hope for a future, when competing expectations from his past were pulling Tony in other directions. He was trying to make his daughter happy and keep relations with his wife civil enough for them to function as co-parents, while struggling to protect me from their hostility. A Facebook profile page was set up in the name of Decca Aitkenhead, not by me but by someone in Malaga. Tony's business relationships required social maintenance, very much as corporate executives need to play golf together, but he had grown more and more disenchanted with the late-night tedium of self-aggrandising anecdotes that passed for conversation. He was also becoming demoralised by the diminishing returns. The wholesale price of cocaine had rocketed, while the street value remained stable, and the dwindling profit margin was making an alternative career look attractive. He wondered what else he might be able to do. The classes he took at the local college had given him an appetite for further study, and an interest in university. We were in the early stages of discussions about applying for a course that could lead him there when he was arrested.

The arrest came out of the blue, on a lazy Sunday afternoon. We had been to the local pub for a roast, and were about to curl up on the sofa to watch a film when my friend Tom, who lived a few streets away, happened to pass by. A few days earlier the teenage boy from next door had told us that his friend was selling a flat-screen TV, and were we interested? We weren't, but when Tony mentioned it to Tom he was, so Tony told me to pause the movie, hopped into Tom's car, and said he would be back in twenty minutes.

When I heard a great commotion in the street about half an hour later, at first I paid no attention. As the shouting grew louder and louder, I recognised Tony's voice. What was going on? I went to the window, and saw Tony sitting on the wall. A short, white, ginger-haired man was standing over him on the pavement, screaming in his face. Who was he? And why was Tony just sitting there letting him? I strained to see further, and could make out half of Tom on the wall near Tony. What I guessed was the television was wrapped in a black bin liner, leaning against the car, and the boot was wide open. As I stared in confusion several more men appeared on the pavement, who seemed to be friends of the little angry redhead. Then I saw the plastic gloves. They were plain-clothes police officers. A moment later a police van pulled up, and Tony and Tom were bundled into the back and driven away.

The following twelve hours cannot have been easy for the custody officer at Kentish Town police station. I phoned continually, demanding information with all the righteous indignation and pompous legalese I could muster, insisting I be allowed to speak to Tony at once. Amazingly, I was. He and I must have talked at least half a dozen times, until in the end I think even he got fed up with the endless calls and said I might as well go to bed and get some sleep. By this point it was established that an unmarked police car had tailed Tom and Tony, thinking they looked unlikely to be friends. Tom is a white middle-class professional who makes television documentaries. After watching them visit a council estate, then a cash point, and return briefly to the estate, they deduced a drug deal was taking place and pulled them over. On finding the TV on the back seat, they assumed it was stolen and arrested both of them. Tom told me later that officers at the station had been rather embarrassed and apologetic about hauling in such an obviously upstanding fellow as himself. There was an awkward moment when swabs were taken from their mouths to test for drugs, and Tony's was negative but Tom tested positive for cocaine. After that, Tom said, they were slightly shorter with him, but he was released without charge a few hours later. Tony was released next morning, having been charged with handling stolen goods.

Any irony in the situation was lost on Tony. Watching

him disappear in the police van, my mind had spun through a catalogue of entirely plausible worst-case scenarios which made prosecution for handling stolen goods practically funny by comparison, but Tony did not see it that way. He was outraged. Once my relief had subsided it was easy to see why, for if he looked like Tom he would almost certainly not now be facing trial at crown court. A conviction seemed inconceivable, but the consequences incalculable just at the point when he was considering a new kind of life. Balanced precariously between past and future, I knew which way a guilty verdict would tip him.

I was worried about how he would come across in the witness box. Tony could be easily provoked by authority, never more so than when he was in the right, and I feared that any half-decent barrister would rattle him. Once Tony started shouting there was no knowing what a jury would infer. I recruited my brother Tom to role-play the trial with Tony, and we spent a series of comical evenings with Tom strutting about the kitchen, 'I put it to you, Mr Wilkinson'-ing, while Tony predictably lost his temper. With each rehearsal the explosions came later and grew milder, until his self-possession was quite impervious to all Tom's insinuations. Still taking no chances, I asked some friends to come along to court and sit in the public gallery so the jury would see he had support, a reliable sign of a serial offender being one for whom no friends or family can be bothered to turn up. Tony thought this was over the top. 'Dec, I've stood trial at the Old Bailey,' he would point out. 'Mmm,' I'd nod. 'And Tone, you got fourteen years.'

He was probably right about the public gallery bit, but I struggled to share his certainty that innocence guaranteed acquittal. As the trial date grew nearer I began to see that his confidence was shakier than he liked to pretend.

On the day the jury took less than an hour to return a verdict of not guilty. We were jubilant. That spring Tony applied to Tower Hamlets College for a full-time access course to study humanities, and was elated to be offered a place. My brother Matt got married, and the estrangement with my family began to thaw. I wasn't ready to bring Tony to the wedding with me, but a few weeks later a family friend in Wiltshire threw a party and we went together. Although not easy at first, relations between Tony and my relatives gradually found their own rhythm, and he grew close to many of them, particularly my brother Tom. The reality of him was altogether less alarming than anything their imaginations had conjured, and although to some he would always remain a mystifying choice, the generosity of his heart was unmistakable to everyone, and impossible not to warm to.

We bought a house in Hackney, and spent the summer renovating it, with Tony the project manager. Under his singular management style the site resembled a cross between Notting Hill Carnival and *Changing Rooms*. It was frenetic and chaotic, and fabulous fun. The work was completed by September, and Tony enrolled in college.

I would not have been at all surprised if he had dropped out in week one. Having abandoned formal education in early adolescence, he was a stranger to academic discipline, and cheerfully confessed to having little idea what he had signed up for. He fortified himself by purchasing industrial quantities of stationery and different-coloured pens and pencils, and set off on day one with enthusiasm. 'Get out of your comfort zone' is a tiresome mantra of self-help manuals, but the degree to which Tony was now leaving his was quite extreme, and having always harboured a fear of public failure I was lost in admiration. I found his dauntlessness poignant, and prayed he hadn't bitten off more than he could chew.

'Dec,' he asked that evening. 'What's a paragraph?' Tony had never written an essay, and had only the haziest notion of what one would involve. In the early weeks we spent the evenings running through the basics. Imagine your essay notes are a supermarket, I suggested. A paragraph is like a shopping basket into which you put one type of produce. Vegetables go in one basket, fruit in another, frozen food in another, and so on. If you have a basket containing radishes, chocolate and flour, something has gone wrong. 'Paragraph = like shopping basket,' he wrote carefully in his notebook, underlining it twice in red for good measure.

Academically, it was always going to be a struggle. What I hadn't factored in was Tony's impact on his tutors, who were enchanted and quickly became good friends. To anyone who works in adult education, the dream student is one whose life they can transform, and in this respect Tony was an infinitely more exciting prospect than the typical intake of early-twentysomething school dropouts. He approached college much as he might a house party, and his noisy enthusiasm secured him the status of campus star. At the end of the year he graduated top of his class, and was chosen to be the poster boy for the college's promotional campaign. His face appeared on billboards across east London. He applied to Westminster University to study psychology and criminology, and was awarded a gold scholarship.

Tony was nervous about becoming an undergraduate. In the first term the intellectual leap panicked him, but again he quickly caught the eye of tutors, one of whom had a hunch he might be dyslexic. A series of tests confirmed the diagnosis, and once equipped with software to assist literacy Tony began to find his feet. Nominated to be the student representative on his course, he took his responsibilities touchingly seriously. Most of the other students on the course were young Muslim women who lived with their parents, and the first few study groups to assemble at our house looked decidedly apprehensive on the doorstep. Tony would lead them upstairs with great trays of food, and before long I would hear shrieks of laughter from the office on the top floor. I could not have been prouder, or more charmed. At the end of his first term we spent Christmas with my family, and flew to Treasure Beach on Boxing Day. I was about to turn thirty-eight. If we were going to have children, now was probably the time. I thought it would take at least a year, but when we got home two weeks later I was pregnant.

Tony was ecstatic. I was terrified. Any concerns about

Tony being the father of my children had vanished long ago; my worry was me. Was I cut out for it? I knew I did not want to not have children, but this wasn't the same as wanting them; I envied the women in parks with dogs instead of prams, and developed a recurring dream about giving birth to a Labrador puppy. Tony's excitement remained undimmed as I gained 6 stone, and my flap about whether I would even love my own baby – 'But why would I? I don't love anyone else's, and mine will be exactly the same as all the rest' – only made him laugh. When Jake was born Tony was a little taken aback, for he was white with blonde hair. Genetic recognition held a particular power for Tony, having been adopted by a family who looked nothing like him, but if I thought Jake's appearance could throw him I was wrong. Nothing meant more to Tony than fatherhood, and his joyful confidence that day taught me how to be a mother. As I dissolved into the traditional puddle of adoration over our beautiful newborn son, he had the good grace not to say I told you so. We named him after Jake's hotel in Treasure Beach.

Over the years I had observed in many new fathers the classic male misgivings – resentment at domestic confinement, alienation from a partner no longer fetching but covered in sour milk, boredom with the never-ending nappies, jealousy at finding their status usurped. Tony would not have thought to call himself a feminist, but unlike so many men who do he was genuinely egalitarian, and none of the constraints or indignities of parenthood troubled him a bit. Given the chance he would have happily taken my maternity leave and sent me back to work. As Jake got older, when Tony took him out strangers would often scoop the blonde white toddler up and demand to know where his parents were. I wouldn't have blamed Tony for minding, but he found it only funny.

In the summer holidays before Jake was born, I had suggested he go and see Camila Batmanghelidjh. She was the founder of Kids Company, a vast and radically progressive charity in London that supported thousands of the capital's most desperately dispossessed children, most of whom had no functional parents and many of whom were heavily involved in crime. I had met Camila through my work, and thought Tony could perhaps do some voluntary work that he could put on his CV. When they met she offered him a job on the spot. Tony was employed for the summer as a high-risk outreach worker to help gang members in south London off the streets and into education or employment. He would continue to work for Kids Company in every university holiday, with a permanent position waiting for him on graduation.

Kids Company closed down a year after Tony died, amid accusations of accounting irregularities and idiosyncratic governance. Having been heavily funded by the government, the charity's closure created quite a public furore, and at the time of writing the conclusions of official investigations are still pending. I do not know what they will find. It is, however, safe to say that had Kids Company operated a more conventionally formal policy of appointments by committee, Tony would almost certainly not have got the job. But Camila understood what a biography like his would bring to the charity's work, and her instincts were not wrong.

His formal job title was 'keyworker', but a more accurate description of the role would be surrogate parent. Whereas statutory social services operate within bureaucratic boundaries and office hours, Tony's involvement in his young clients' lives was limitlessly intimate, extending into every chaotic detail. If a boy refused to go to school, Tony would show up early each morning, get him out of bed, drive him to school, walk him to class, and if necessary even sit with him through his lessons. When a youngster needed a winter coat or warm shoes, Tony would take him clothes shopping. Defeated by the complexity of council housing applications, many of his clients were homeless, so Tony would steer them through the byzantine process, then help decorate and furnish their flats. Ungovernable pet dogs – pit bulls, usually – were a recurring challenge, requiring delicate negotiations to relinquish ownership to the RSPCA. In a typical working day Tony could advocate on behalf of one client in court, visit another in prison, apply for an apprenticeship, mediate in a row with a girlfriend, and take a carload of teenagers out to the cinema.

Having never had a job before, Tony was unfamiliar with the etiquette of formal employment. He went around telling everyone he knew how much he earned, and was puzzled by others' reluctance to disclose their salaries in return. As Tony's was a fraction of his former income, one might have thought he would rather keep it to himself. The new role of junior breadwinner would be a confronting adjustment for anyone to make, and of course he did not like it. Had his masculinity been any less secure, it would have been dangerously destabilising; had his ability to accommodate change been more like most of ours, it could have been impossible. But Tony had the most astonishing capacity to reconcile himself to new realities, and the cheerful dignity with which he accepted his reduced financial power was remarkable.

Tony's willingness to change was one of the things that made him so good at his job. It is a tall order to turn up on a council estate and win the trust of impenetrably wary and often armed gang members. It is an even taller order to persuade them to suspend their suspicions and risk a different kind of life. Their resistance was entirely rational, based on a lifetime of overwhelming evidence that society did not want them, and had Tony's faith in their potential been no more than an abstract ideal of liberal theory, I doubt he would have got very far. But he believed they could change because he had, and the respect his credibility commanded was literally life-changing for many of the young men he worked with.

Kids Company was founded on the philosophy that what every child needs, more than anything else, is to feel loved. The youngsters Tony worked with had known only neglect and abuse. His love for them was authentically unconditional, because he recognised so much of himself in their damage, and I recognised something of myself in its impact on them. No matter how many times my head had told me, in the early years with Tony, that our relationship was doomed and I should walk away, the force of his love had overpowered reason and compelled me to stay. Even then, for a long time I had still thought his faith in our future was fundamentally flawed. A romantic dream was lovely, but no contest for logic, and in the long run my intellectual analysis of our incompatibility would have to prevail. Now I was forced to concede that he had been right all along, and I was wrong. Love really had been enough to make anything possible.

What neither education nor a career could ever do was make Tony middle-class. When we first met, class was such an unfamiliar concept to Tony that he scarcely knew what the word even meant, for he had interpreted his life entirely through the prism of race, and the criminal class to which he had always belonged eludes conventional classification. This made him a more authentic class refugee than either Paul or I, and was both enormously attractive to me and an inexhaustible source of potential confusion. Many of my cultural expectations and assumptions were even more alien to Tony than they had been to my ex-husband. But whereas Paul had found them threatening, to Tony they were merely baffling, as anthropologically exotic as his criminal class codes were to me.

The convention of false modesty was a mystery to him. Why would anyone pretend to be bad at something they were good at? He assumed that self-deprecation would be taken at face value, and as he would rather be thought well of it struck him as much more sensible to tell people how brilliant he was. There was no limit to Tony's boasting; it was quite shameless, and could be extravagant to the point of baroque. I feared it could only achieve the opposite of its intended effect, but nothing I said could convince Tony that bragging about his talents might cause others to doubt them. My refusal to refer to him as 'Daddy' – as in, 'Jake, give the bottle to Daddy,' or 'Daddy's home!' thoroughly bemused him. My explanation that it was anathema to my very faintly counter-cultural class made no sense to him, but after a while Jake began calling him Tony too, and in due course gave up calling me Mum and opted for Decca instead. I don't think Tony ever really liked it, but he was wise enough to see that insisting upon Daddy would be pedantic, and probably futile anyway.

His critique of other social codes was illuminating. For example, I was brought up to preface any request for a favour with a long list of reasons why it might justifiably be declined, because it was good manners to make it easy for the other person to say no. Tony found this bizarre. If you want the answer to be yes, why go out of your way to invite no? When I began to notice that Tony got what he wanted far more frequently than I did, I came to see his point.

He was similarly bewildered by my obligation to display elaborate interest in the health of our Albanian cleaner's extended family. I would dutifully tidy up before she arrived, then spend hours soliciting updates on the various ailments afflicting her husband's second cousin in Pristina, or her grandmother's hip replacement, under the misapprehension that this would convey respect and make her like me. Tony's policy was altogether more successful. He would lie in bed like a sultan while she cleaned around him, and dispatch her to the kitchen to make him cups of coffee. I stopped dying of embarrassment when it became abundantly clear that she was much fonder of him than of me. 'Oooh, Tony, you are so funny!' she would giggle affectionately.

What was tactlessly rude in my eyes was often, I came to see, surprisingly winning. A painfully shy young man on Tony's course consulted him for advice about how to approach a student he fancied. Tony's response made my hair stand on end. 'Listen, mate, there's no point even talking to her till you sort out your teeth. They're a bloody mess, mate, they look awful.' A few weeks later the man knocked at our door again. He had come to say thank you. Having followed Tony's advice and taken himself off to a dentist, his teeth were now sparkling white, and he was taking the girl out on a date that night. 'You are a true friend,' he beamed, hugging Tony.

The differences that used to make our relationship feel untenable now seemed to make life with Tony endlessly interesting. In some respects, however, the gulf would always remain so unbridgeable that at times it seemed a miracle we were still together. Like most criminals, Tony's relationship with money had always been impulsive and carelessly chaotic. The chancy nature of illicit earnings is notoriously unconducive to financial planning, and vast sums would be lavished away as quickly as they appeared.

A fixed monthly salary had no impact whatsoever on his inability to budget, and the recklessness of his attitude to debt drove me mad. Likewise, no amount of education would alter the fundamental way his mind worked. Tony's thought process would never be academic or analytic, and he found it impossible to distinguish empirically based beliefs from desires. If you asked him if he thought it would rain tomorrow, his reply would have nothing to do with the Met Office forecast, and everything to do with whether or not he wanted the sun to shine.

The fact that his opinions turned out to be right more often than logic or the laws of probability could explain did not necessarily help, and begged a disconcerting question. Would it be more rewarding to be with someone who was more often wrong than right, but reached his faulty conclusions via a cognitive route I could relate to? I could never be sure. When Malcolm Gladwell's book *Blink* came out, Tony was nonplussed by its excitable reception among the intelligentsia. Its revelations of how small a part intellectual analysis plays in most human decisions struck him as stating the obvious. We went to hear the author talk, and afterwards he was quite sniffy. 'What's the big deal? He's just describing how I think. I could have written that book.' But I think he was gratified to find the workings of his mind recognised by an esteemed professor. They still remained a mystery to me. I could not understand how anyone could enjoy *The Sopranos* and *The Transformers* in equal measure, or deny any contrast in quality. But I could see that if the choice is between critical discernment and non-judgemental pleasure, the latter might well take the prize.

Tony's determination to enjoy himself was contagious, and made me a sunnier version of myself than I would have believed possible. The second pregnancy was a surprise – I had only been back at work a month from maternity leave – but this time I trusted Tony's enthusiasm, and in the spring of 2011 Joe was born. We were beside ourselves with joy. Weeks later Tony graduated from university with a first. In full mortar-board and gown regalia, he wore an expression of such unbridled triumph as he received his certificate that a great gale of cheers and laughter erupted across the hall. That Christmas we took the boys to Treasure Beach, and by the end of the holiday we had bought a piece of land in the village, and begun plans to build a house.

After all the dissonance and fracture of our early years, at last we seemed to make sense. The jigsaw pieces of our separate lives had reassembled themselves into a coherent identity, and created a family that felt like home. Sometimes the consonance felt almost uncanny. Tony's background made him perfect for Kids Company; his job made him heroic to my world; becoming parents together had made us happier than we could have dreamed. The misfit class identity which had looked like such a problem for so long had led me to someone who turned out to embody liberal ideals of equality, human potential and tolerance more authentically than most of the middle-class lefties I know who talk a good game, including myself.

In May 2013 we sold our house in Hackney and bought

a dilapidated old farmhouse in rural Kent. Having never been able to see myself raising a family in the city, I wanted the open fields and freedom of my childhood for our boys. Tony was equally enthusiastic, and the house hunt began in high spirits. After several dispiriting months I was beginning to wonder if finding a countryside idyll within commuting distance of work was a fantasy. Were we even cut out for country life, anyway? Tony was blithely undaunted by the prospect of being the only non-white face for miles, but I worried that he might have underestimated the depth of rural prejudice.

All doubts vanished the day we found Tubslake. Overgrown and ungentrified, the timber-frame house was a beguiling muddle of beams and inglenook fireplaces surrounded by an ancient oasthouse, three dilapidated barns, an enormous piggery and meadowland. Our hearts were lost before we reached the front door. After six long anxious months of negotiations, it was ours. We packed our old life into a removals lorry and set off in a daze of blissful disbelief. I thought we were the luckiest family alive.

The boys were enchanted by their new world of bluebells and badgers, trees and dens. Tony was delirious with excitement, bursting with schemes for chickens, pigs and orchards, and made friends with half the neighbourhood within months of moving in. He began plans to convert the barns into dormitories and classrooms, and create an educational farm for Kids Company youngsters to escape to. 'I've got everything I ever wanted,' he took to marvelling. Soon so did I. A less auspicious beginning to our life together would have been difficult to script, and yet everything precious to me I now owed to him.

For years after leaving my marriage, I had had a nagging doubt that nothing I built with Tony could ever be more than second-best. 'Dec,' he remarked one day, as we lay in bed. 'If we had both signed up for internet dating sites, what algorithm in the world would have matched us up?' Any website as insane as that, I agreed, would probably be sued, and both of us laughed. But against all reasonable expectations, we had made it.

5

As the news of Tony's death flies through Treasure Beach, villagers descend upon Calabash Cottage, bursting into the bedroom in breathless disbelief. Voices are clamouring, yelling, murmuring; I perch on the foot of the bed rocking. In the pandemonium Jake and Joe are led away to the villa next door. Someone hands me a Valium. The police arrive and want Tony's passport; when they hand it back an hour later it is wrapped in a plastic bag containing his watch and gold chain. Tony has become a body. I become dimly aware that the policemen are expecting me to give a statement, until the indignant crowd shoos them out of the cottage.

I have often wondered which of my friends I would phone on *Who Wants to Be a Millionaire?*, but never considered which one I would call first in a catastrophe. The answer turns out to be none of them. It is my three brothers I call first – Tom in Hackney, Ben in Manhattan and then Matt in Gloucestershire, who has already been told and is sobbing down the line when he answers. Someone hands me a phone, and I find myself talking to my ex-husband in London, who has heard the news from a friend in the village. After speaking to my father in Wiltshire, the friend I phone is the journalist Jenni Russell.

I don't know what to say to them, because the truth sounds like a lie. I see now why formulaic preambles such as Are you sitting down? are useful, because otherwise a sudden death is impossible to announce without sounding out of your mind. Even as I start to speak, I know it will sound like madness. All I can say, over and over, is: 'Tony's drowned. He's lying on the beach, he's dead. He's just lying there dead.' Jenni doesn't even know we're in Jamaica when she answers her phone. She asks if I want her to come, and I expect to say of course not, but what comes out of my mouth is: 'Yes. Come, please come.' The audacity of my need shocks me. Already, I am becoming unrecognisable to myself.

People keep crowding into the cottage. I have lost all track of time when our friend Laura, the wife of Jason, who owns Jake's, packs a bag of clothes and drives us away to their house in the mountains. Jake and Joe are silent in the back seat of the car, pale and bewildered. I have to clench my hands between my knees to stop myself flinging open the door and jumping out. I cannot believe we are simply abandoning Tony; how can we leave him there like that? I know I can't run back to him on the beach, I know others are taking care of his body, I know I have to stay with Jake and Joe. But to get in a car and drive away feels like unspeakable betrayal.

At Laura's house Jake and Joe play with her children with a vacant air of detachment that reminds me of sleepwalkers. I drift from room to room in a Valium haze, restless and disorientated; Jenni tells me later that we spoke several times on the phone, but I have no recollection. Friends from the village arrive, and we sit at the long wooden table on the veranda, gazing out over the vastness of the distant ocean. In London a friend tells Tony's nineteen-year-old daughter that he has died. Just before midnight Ben arrives from New York.

Ben is the eldest brother, six years older than me, and six foot eight tall. When we were children he was the sensible, serious one – our father called it 'first child-itis', but we called him a young fogey, and liked to make fun of his self-appointed seniority. He graduated from Oxford, moved to New York, became a Wall Street banker, married an Ivy League doctor and in due course ascended to elite membership of the Upper East Side's 0.01 per cent while the rest of us were still falling about in nightclubs. At forty-nine he is the most grown-up grown-up I know, and when his arms fold around me I can almost believe everything will be alright. I crumple into bed, weak with relief that Ben is here. Jake is asleep beside me; in the morning, for the first time in his life he has wet the bed.

We awake to clouds so low and heavy that the entire house is swaddled in mist. It's like being in an aeroplane. Jake and Joe seem curiously unsurprised by Ben's arrival, and play together so unselfconsciously that I wonder if they could have blanked the previous day's memory. Then Joe spots Tony's phone on a sofa.

'That's Tony's phone,' he says.

'Yes,' says Jake. 'But he died. I walked into the sea, and he died saving me.'

'Oh yeah,' Joe says. 'So does that mean we can play on his phone?'

Someone tells me that a newspaper in London, *The Times*, has already called Jake's, asking for details of Tony's death. I am thrown – not least because ever since we left Calabash Cottage, a lie has been circling in my mind. Was Jake clear about exactly what happened – and might he in time forget? Would it be kinder to let him grow up being told a story of how Tony drowned that spared him any risk of misplaced guilt? I have never had much interest in rigid rules for parenting, but honesty has always seemed so obviously important that a self-imposed prohibition against lying would have seemed laughably unnecessary. I am shocked by the temptation to lie to my own son. It is a relief that the truth will be printed in black and white, and I can no longer succumb to the allure of deceit.

At lunchtime Annabelle calls to say that a British couple who have heard the news would like to lend us their beach villa, Minerva, a few miles west of Treasure Beach. Someone from Jake's packs up our belongings at Calabash

Cottage. In the afternoon Laura drives us to Minerva, and late that night Tom, Matt, Jenni and Danielle, my children's former nanny and a dear friend, fly in from London.

Minerva is a glamorous James Bond beach villa overlooking a private bay. The visitors' book opens with Lily Allen's name. It is a bizarre place for us to gather, dazed with jetlag and grief, but I am ashamed to realise that even in this state I'm secretly pleased Minerva will make Treasure Beach look desirable to the others. I feel inexplicably defensive about this place I have loved for so long; I want the others to love it too, or at least to see why I do. I cannot believe I care; it's absurd, almost insane. But I don't want them to blame Treasure Beach for Tony's death. Or perhaps it's that I don't want them to blame me, for bringing him to the place that has taken his life.

Survivors' guilt is a lot like 'This happens to other people' – another trope of the typical post-tragedy tale with which I have always been impatient. Why do people always think someone else's death was their fault – and that if they had only acted differently, they could have prevented it? The illogic has always been baffling to me, and the implicit self-importance rather alienating. But by the time my brothers and friends have arrived, I am convinced they are furious with me for killing Tony. Because in my mind I did.

We sit up late that first night, around the glass dining table on the terrace, and I tell them the story of how Tony died. It takes for ever, because I keep breaking down. The expression in their eyes as they listen looks to me like blame

– because how could I have let this happen? How could I have allowed Tony to die? It will be days before I begin to see that what feels and looks like guilt is not really guilt at all, but something quite different.

I do not yet understand this on our first night in Minerva. It feels perfectly obvious that everyone is silently blaming me anyway, so I might as well acknowledge the truth. I should have warned Tony about the undertow when he headed down to the beach, I blurt out desperately. I should have told him not to let Jake near the water. When I saw Jake in the waves, why didn't I scream at Tony to stay out of the water? He didn't have to rescue Jake – I'm sure I could have got there in time to save him. Or if only I had swum straight out to them both, instead of waiting until they were in trouble. Tony would have had enough strength to fight the current and get back to shore. Why didn't I swim back out to him once Jake was safe? I could have reached him before the others did, I'm sure I could.

But worst of all – far worse than all of that – why didn't I panic? When I swam to him in the water, why did it not occur to me that his life was in danger? Tony was dying in front of my eyes, and I didn't even panic.

As I register the table's astonishment at my outburst, I do not believe it for one second. They are just pretending; they're pretending to look surprised, they're pretending it is not what they have all been thinking. Suddenly everyone is talking at once. I cannot be serious, they are saying. I can't mean what I'm saying. It's sheer lunacy – can't I see it's insane? I must be out of my mind.

When I realise they actually mean it, I do not feel relieved. I feel exasperated and let down. What is wrong with them all? I don't care if it takes a shouting match to make them see I am right, and am about to start yelling across the table when Tom intervenes, sparing us what would have undoubtedly been the most bizarre argument in our family history. Slowly and softly, as if addressing a small child, he talks me through each flaw in my logic. I am having none of it – until he gets to the point about panic.

'If you'd panicked, Dec,' he says gently, 'we wouldn't all be sitting here now. We would have come to Jamaica to bring Joe home, because he would have been an orphan. The only reason you and Jake are still alive now is because you didn't panic. You saved Jake's life.'

I am silenced. The idea that Jake might have drowned too had not entered my mind. Tom reaches across, takes my hand, and stares at me. 'Dec, there was nothing you could do. There was nothing anybody could do. There was literally nothing you or anyone else could have done to save Tony's life.' And suddenly, I know this is true.

But where is the relief? I should be flooded with it. Only I am not. What happens instead is that I see in my mind Tony's body on Calabash beach. Annabelle is kneeling over him; crowds are gathered around him on the sand. Seagulls circle overhead. Sunlight sparkles in the waves. But heavy velvet curtains frame the scene, for the beach has turned into a stage set – and as I hear Tom say there was nothing anyone could have done, the stage lights slowly dim and fade away until there is nothing left but darkness. The play is over, and I am swallowed up by despair.

When I awake next morning, the first thought that enters my head is: Oh my God, if we'd kept to the original plan and spent week two of the holiday in the other cottage I had booked, Tony would still be alive! This thought is quickly abandoned when I remember it was actually Tony's idea to stay put in Calabash Cottage, not mine. But the holiday itself had been my idea! My mind races back to our living-room sofa in Kent on a rainy night in March, and my fatal suggestion: 'I know this is a crazy idea, Tone, but I reckon we should go to Jamaica.' And because of those words, Tony is dead.

For that matter, if I hadn't moved to Ainsworth Road in the first place he would still be alive. If only Paul and I had bought one of the other houses we viewed all those years ago, Tony and I would never have met and this would not have happened. Whichever way you look at it, there can be no doubt. If it wasn't for me, he wouldn't be dead.

Were this to carry on for days, at some point I imagine Tom's patience would have to snap. It must be bewildering to reason with someone so implacably hostile to reason. Even I can see that I am becoming increasingly irrational, but cannot control this insatiable, rampaging narrative of guilt. I am puzzling over the inexplicable appeal of self-blame, when suddenly it makes sense.

All of my fantasy scenarios present the hypothetical possibility of an outcome in which Tony does not die. In Tom's version of events, nothing could be done to prevent his death. There is no hope. In my guilt-ridden alternatives, on the other hand, the most modest of plot alterations is enough to offer an outcome in which he lives. I am not really feeling guilty at all. I'm just imagining a parallel universe in which Tony does not have to die, one for which taking the blame is a small price to pay, if the alternative is blameless but hopeless despair. We call this survivor's guilt, because it manifests as guilt, but it is really hope. The frantic, primitive desperation of hope.

My own mind is no longer reliable, but there is one thing I do know we have to do. Not for a second since walking away from Tony on the beach have I been alone. Meanwhile Tony has been abandoned to the custody of strangers, and the cruelty of his loneliness is tormenting me. We must go and see him.

I do not know how official channels are supposed to work in Jamaica, because in my experience no one ever uses them. Laura's husband Jason is the person everyone goes to when anything goes wrong; Tony used to joke that Jason was Treasure Beach's unofficial mayor, and now he becomes our unofficial consulate adviser. At breakfast Ben calls him to ask when we can visit Tony's body. When he hangs up I can see the news is bad.

'Dec I'm so sorry,' Ben explains gently. 'We're not allowed to see Tony until they've done the autopsy. And they can't say when that will be.'

'But he doesn't belong to them!' I start to protest. But the intransigence of Jamaican bureaucracy is, I'd learned years ago, quite impervious to uppity tourists' indignation.

Not to see Tony's body would be unthinkable; to see him disfigured and decomposed is unimaginable. But at what point will Tony stop looking like Tony and start looking like a corpse? Do we have days? Weeks? The collective sum of intelligence and education assembled around this breakfast table would give most boardrooms a run for their money, but no one, it quickly transpires, has any idea what happens to a body after death. The phone rings; it's Jason again. When Ben hangs up this time he is shaking his head wryly.

'Who knows how Jason's worked this, but we can go now. We have to have a police escort, and we won't be allowed to touch him, but if we want to see Tony we need to go now.'

Tony's body has been taken to Bent's funeral home in a hillside village a few miles above Treasure Beach. It is a curious-looking building, perched precariously on a hairpin bend, with oval-shaped windows that have always looked to me like eyes, and seemed a surprising architectural choice given Jamaicans' propensity for superstition. I must have driven past the place a thousand times. The thought that it could ever mean anything to me had never entered my head.

We pull up outside in two cars. The police are already there, waiting on the verge; they look awkward, embarrassed perhaps, and do not meet my eye. I leave Jake and Joe with Danielle in a car, and we climb the steps to the reception.

I do not know what I had been expecting, but it

certainly isn't this. Funeral kitsch is widely favoured in Jamaica, and no amount of rococo bling and satin would have surprised me. But a member of staff leads us down some stairs into what looks like an underground car park. Ben has to hold me up as we descend. The police walk ahead of us, and lead us towards a metal trolley in a corner. It looks like a hospital gurney, and on it is lying a white body bag – the kind in which your dry cleaners might return a ball gown. An officer unzips the bag to the waist, and lying there inside it is Tony.

My legs buckle and I cling to Ben. I do not know why the police have waited until now to photograph Tony, but this is the moment they choose to produce a camera and begin taking pictures of his body. It is inexplicable. We turn our backs and look away in silence until they finish, and then very slowly, practically on tiptoe, we inch to Tony's side.

He looks exactly as he always does when asleep. He is still wearing the purple vest and navy shorts he had pulled on just two mornings ago. I want to seize him, shake him, shout at him to wake up, but I am paralysed. 'I'm so sorry, Tony, I'm so sorry,' I try to say, but tears I have not cried since I was a child convulse me. I move to touch his hand, before a policeman barks: 'You cannot touch him! This is a crime scene.' Is it? I do not know what he means.

Thirty-three years ago, the body my brothers and I gathered around in a funeral parlour was our mother's. I do not know if it is that memory which doubles them over in Bent's. I can only think of Tony's two sons in the car outside. After a few minutes I wipe my face, compose myself, and step outside into the sunlight. 'Would you like to come and see Tony?' I say gently, opening the car door. 'It's okay, it's not scary or spooky. He just looks like he's asleep.'

'No!' Jake scowls. 'I don't want to. I'm not coming.' He glares at me angrily. Joe is already quietly climbing out of the car, taking my hand. 'Decca I want to come.' So I lift him into my arms and carry him inside, amazed by the calm I can confect as we reach Tony's side. I'm not even sure if this sudden conjuring trick of self-control is selflessly heroic, or possibly unhealthy. 'He looks just like he's sleeping, doesn't he?' I say softly. Joe gazes down at his father in thoughtful silence. 'Yes, he does,' is all he eventually says.

After leaving Bent's we go for lunch at Jake's. It's my idea. Tom and Matt have been to Treasure Beach before, but I need Jenni and Ben and Danielle to see its beauty and charm, largely indiscernible from the unlovely village lane but framed like a postcard from Jake's poolside restaurant. As soon as we arrive, I see this is a mistake. We look all wrong. My brothers have always been absurdly handsome – Ben looks like one of those flawless American sports stars, Matt looks like Val Kilmer, Tom like a gay male model. Under normal circumstances here they would be taken for glamorously A-list guests. Right now they look more like secret service bodyguards, grim-faced behind black sunglasses in a tense huddle by the pool, and too late it hits me that we must be the last thing Jason could want in his hotel. We are an affront to all this tropical bliss – a morbid caravan of doom – and it is a relief to retreat to the privacy of Minerva.

Like any group of adults thrown together under one roof, we are falling into roles that configure an approximation of a family unit. The four siblings have not spent this long together without partners or children since we were teenagers, and we are no longer the rivals we once were. Instinctively the younger three defer to Ben, who quietly assumes the father role. Matt's adult identity has been defined by playful charisma and explosive sex appeal, and in the absence of an outlet for either he quickly regresses to teasing Ben, but the needling feels perfunctory and has lost its adolescent bite. Tom was always the dissident brother, the provocateur. (When Matt and Ben joined a gym in their teens: 'So in your free time you pay to go into a room where you pick up pieces of metal and put them down again?') He and I used to fight like foxes, but since our twenties he has been my closest confidant, and this status confers on him an unfamiliar authority over his older brothers.

I am a half-presence within the group, sometimes able to play with the boys in the pool, or join the others for a meal, but then a wave of grief will engulf me and I stumble to my room in tears. Now that I am helplessly childlike, all three become the protective brothers people often assume they had always been. In truth, we were never very kind to each other as children. There was more than a touch of

Lord of the Flies in our household after our mum died, and I think we are all taken aback by the tenderness we now find in each other.

Motherless for decades, we are not looking for a surrogate figure, but although Jenni is barely older than Ben, the fearlessness of her intimacy and sheer force of intellect quickly consign her to the role. I first met Jenni at a media party a decade ago, and she has become something between a sister and a mentor to me; formidably self-possessed, she always seems to know what to do. Danielle is the quietest in the group. Tony had known her since she was sixteen, and now at twenty-nine she feels like a younger cousin, a patiently soothing presence for Jake and Joe, who have become unrecognisable to us. They are volatile, clingy, aggressive, erratic, unreadable, and none of us has any idea how to predict or manage their explosions. In a particularly hysterical fit of screams one afternoon, Jake shouts at Tom, 'It is all my fault! It's my fault. Tony died because I walked into the sea.'

I suspect Jake has learnt from me to camouflage sadness or fear as anger. For as long as I can remember, this is how I have always managed pain, so I'm confused by my immunity to anger now that something truly terrible has happened. Matt's rage is more recognisable. He is furious with the sea, and furious with Treasure Beach; why don't they have life guards, why aren't warning signs everywhere? When Ben slips off to the beach alone for a sunset swim, Matt is beside himself. 'How could he? How could he? I tell you what, I'm never fucking stepping foot in the ocean ever again.' The high commission in Kingston calls to say that a relative of Tony's is driving them mad, and can we persuade her to stop calling them. She is calling the *Guardian* too, screaming at my editors.

Tom is obsessed with the forensic details of the death – he needs to know distances, times, and as I struggle to provide them I realise how impossibly unreal it must sound. He wants to see where Tony died, to understand what happened, so when Laura takes the boys to her house one afternoon to play with her children, I take my three brothers back to Calabash beach.

I have to look away as we pass the gate on the lane that leads to Calabash Cottage. We park further along, near the fishing boats, and I lead my brothers across the sand. The water is glassily still once more, and even to me it seems inconceivable that this languid bay could have taken Tony's life. We wade all the way out to the spot where I think he had been when Michael and I began to haul him in, and still we are no more than waist-deep.

On the way back to Minerva we see Blouser outside a small wooden bar on the lane near Jake's, and pull over. He is drunk and incoherent, so we just hug. We stop again when we pass Natty, another of the men who tried to save Tony. I have known Natty for years, and never seen him like this. He is shaky, too jittery to make much sense or eye contact. But later Tom tells me what Natty managed to say after I had got back in the car.

Natty is convinced Tony died of a heart attack. When he, Shugoo and the third man, a fisherman, had reached

Tony in the water, they told him he was safe – 'You're okay now, bro', we've got you. You're safe now.' Tony told them, 'I'm not going to make it.' He asked if Jake was safe. Moments later they felt his body go limp in their arms. Tony died while Michael and I were pulling him in; he was dead before he reached the shore.

Soon it becomes apparent that the whole village is hoping it was a heart attack. Even though his death was nobody's fault, a heart attack will make everyone feel better. It will probably make me feel better too. But all the press reports have portrayed him as a hero who drowned saving his son's life, and I realise I will be embarrassed if this turns out to have been technically untrue.

But how could Tony have drowned without even going under? When Annabelle visits Minerva she tells us about something called dry drowning. The others are puzzled; they have never heard of it. But it rings a vague bell to me, and when we Google it I remember why.

Minerva is one of the few Treasure Beach rental villas I've never stayed in. But I have been here once before. Tony and I were invited to a party here when Jake was barely a toddler and Joe not yet born. I hadn't given the party a thought in years, but my memory of that day is now so freighted with premonition that as I recount it to the others I can barely believe it myself.

We had been leaving the party when we paused at the poolside to chat with Jason. Quite how Jake toppled into the pool as we were talking I can't recall, but I do remember Tony's reaction. Jake had barely hit the water before he hurled himself in, and with Jake safely in his arms had clambered back out wearing an expression to suggest he had just saved his son from certain death. It seemed such a melodramatic overreaction that Jason had half-laughed. With an affectionate pat on Tony's dripping back, he said something like, 'Cool yourself, man.'

Tony spun around, incensed. 'Don't you know just a teaspoon of water can kill? That's all it takes. If he inhaled just a teaspoon of water, it would be enough to kill him.' I remember I felt embarrassed by his outburst, and frankly doubtful it could even be remotely true. And now here we are, gathered around my laptop in Minerva, discovering he was absolutely right. You don't have to be underwater to drown. Tony's lungs had filled with water while he had been floundering in the waves, gasping for air and calling for help.

But until an autopsy has been conducted, no one can know for sure if this really is how he died. At first we are told that it may be six weeks before the autopsy takes place, but Jason intervenes again, and suddenly the authorities inform us that it will happen on Monday, just days after Tony's death. When Monday morning comes, Joe asks me what day it is. I tell him, and his next question confuses me. Will it hurt, he asks, when they get on top of Tony? Will they hurt him? I can't think what he means, until I realise that he has overheard us discussing something called an autopsy, which will happen on Monday. Joe has no idea what an autopsy is; what he has heard sounds to him that on Monday people are going to get on top of

Tony; they will be 'on top of he'. And so Joe wonders if it will hurt.

He keeps asking if we can go back to see Tony again, 'to check if he has come back alive'. This sounds like a perfectly sensible suggestion to me, because I do not believe he is never coming back. My self-image of a rational, logical empiricist is proving to be wildly inaccurate, for it is becoming evident that I am scarcely any more rational than a witch doctor. What I know to be true, and what I actually believe, turn out to be poles apart.

I believe Tony is about to walk through Minerva's door at any minute.

When I wake up four days after he died, I look at the clock and realise it is exactly the time when we should have been arriving home in Kent. It says so in my diary; we should be in our house by now, and in my mind that means it must be true. I had written it down, hadn't I? If it is written in the diary then in my mind what is happening instead literally cannot be real.

I am beginning to see that most of my notions of reality are really just figments of my imagination, nothing more than plans I have made and mistaken for truths. For all my Western education, the Jamaicans in Treasure Beach have an infinitely clearer understanding of reality than mine. They already knew that life was unpredictable and precarious, and are not dumbfounded by sudden death. One evening they hold a memorial for Tony at the cricket pavilion. I do not want to go; I don't think I will be able to bear it, but am glad when I do. A young man I have known since he was an infant plays African drums, and Jason's aunt, an elderly and devout Christian, sings an old West Indian slave song, 'I'll Fly Away'. Jason makes a speech about Tony; Ben thanks the village for its support. We all eat jerk chicken and drink Red Stripe as the sun sets.

When Annabelle told me that Tony was dead, I couldn't think beyond Treasure Beach. In my mind, the tragedy belonged to the village. The only other person I had thought about beyond that was Tony's daughter. The rest of the world might as well not have existed. How wrong I was about that becomes apparent very quickly, as I discover the surreal experience of becoming a newspaper story.

The first press call to Jake's had come within hours of Tony's death, and newspapers keep calling. I had been confused: why were they interested? But of course, this is 'a story', so I had knelt at a laptop on Laura's veranda and drafted an account, which the press report as 'a statement released by the family'. It doesn't feel like a statement to me; it still feels like an impossible untruth. The *Guardian* wants to run an obituary, and Jenni makes a start on one, until she panics about what the *Daily Mail* will do when it discovers that this man being portrayed by the media as a hero was in fact once a criminal. Who knows what dirt they might gleefully dig up? Jenni's instinct is unequivocal; we must tell the *Guardian* to abandon the obituary idea at once.

My feelings are more ambivalent. They are also naïve. Surely, I say, the *Mail* would never do that to me and my family? Jenni snorts. She is right, of course – but I struggle to conceal my disappointment. I want to pretend that the media interest in Tony's death is irksome and unwelcome – but the truth is, it isn't. I find it hard to admit, even to myself, how gratifying it is to see his death so widely reported. I want to pretend that this is only because I know how pleased Tony would have been – and it is true that he would have been. But to pass off my own pleasure as purely vicarious would be a lie. I don't know why the media coverage matters to me. All I know is that it does.

And yet at the same time I worry about its legacy for Jake. When he is old enough to read the reports about his father's heroic sacrifice, will he feel comforted and proud, or resentful? I don't want him burdened by some sense that he has to live up to the saintliness of a ghost dreamt up by hacks.

One consequence of the press coverage I had not anticipated is the deluge of emails and text messages that begin pouring in. Many are from close friends, or people I know well. Some are from celebrities I have only ever met when I interviewed them. I would like to say that the messages from the famous people mean little to me – but again, that would be a lie. I am astounded, and mildly horrified, by my gratification.

I wish my embarrassment regarding these emails ended there, but it doesn't. One arrives from an immensely wealthy Jamaican businessman called Butch Stewart, who owns the Sandals hotel chain, and for many years also owned the Air Jamaica airline. We have met several times through work, and have always got along, but I couldn't claim to be his friend. So I am surprised and moved to receive an email from him, forwarded on by various intermediaries, conveying his condolences and asking if he can help in any way. My big mistake is to read this email aloud during dinner.

'Jesus, Dec, he's a billionaire!' exclaims Matt at once. 'Dec, he is a bill-i-on-aire! Can he help? Of course he can! He can send you a sum of money big enough to change your life, and too small for him to even notice on his bank statement. Dec! I'm serious! For fuck's sake, email him back and ask him for some money.'

Once again, what I would like to say at this point would not actually be true. I don't tell Matt he is being vulgar or greedy. I laugh. I haven't laughed since Tony died, and it feels startling and miraculous, like breaking out of prison. As soon as I stop, the only thought in my head is how nice it would be to escape again.

I would still have had the good sense to stop the joke going any further, had a friend from the village not then happened to drop by and handed me a spliff.

I have never been a big fan of cannabis. I don't need a drug to make me vague and a bit careless; I can manage that quite easily by myself. But every now and then I still give it a go, because very occasionally I get a pleasant surprise, and it makes me giggly and silly instead of sleepy. This, regrettably, is one of those occasions.

What happens next is a measure of our collective derangement, and later a source of such embarrassment to some that it would be unfair to specify precisely who says what. But somebody produces a laptop, and in this unexpected delirium of laughter we begin to dictate what we imagine to be a subtly lucrative reply. The ridiculous email is still being drafted when I make my next mistake. Butch isn't the only billionaire, I announce with a giggle, who has been in touch to offer help. I am slightly taken aback by the impact of this revelation. The table freezes.

'What do you mean?' someone asks, suddenly alarmingly serious.

'Um, well, I had one from David Furnish too. You know, Elton John's husband.' The table erupts.

I expect Danielle to find all this shameless avarice distasteful. She is an actual Christian, for a start, and the most fastidiously virtuous person I know, who grew up on a council estate in Hackney, has worked hard all her life, but at twenty-nine still can't afford to move out to a place of her own. To Danielle perhaps we all look like billionaires. But when I glance at her, she too is laughing and nodding vigorously.

And so, to my eternal mortification, we send off an email to the two billionaires, thanking them for their generous offer of help and suggesting it might best be realised in a monetary form. By now I am so stoned that I consider these emails to be both elegantly tasteful and guaranteed to generate substantial piles of cash. There is no doubt in my mind – until I awake the next morning. Oh my God. What can we have been thinking? What must they have thought when they opened these emails? To this day I do not know the answer, because – unsurprisingly – I never heard from either one again.

All I want to do is go home. But we are not leaving until we can bring Tony's body with us, and Jamaican bureaucracy proceeds at a snail's pace. My brothers cajole and harass and chivvy, and Jason applies more pressure, and eventually – eight days later – we are allowed to take Tony home.

An old friend drives us north across the mountains to Montego Bay. I have had to introduce the boys to a whole new vocabulary of death – undertaker, hearse, coffin, funeral – and explained that Tony's body will be on the same plane as us. I think I have taken care to make sure they understand it all, until Jake asks how we will carry Tony onto the plane; he thinks the body will be propped in a seat next to us. Joe asks if we can please go straight home when the plane lands, and not 'to the party for everyone who love Tony'. I have explained that when we get back to England there will be a funeral – 'a sort of party for everyone who loved Tony' – so he assumes it will take place that very day. Losing heart in my ability to make any useful sense to them, when we pass a Bent's hearse driving south and I realise it must have carried Tony to the airport that morning, I do not point it out.

In the departures hall at Montego Bay airport I unravel into a monstrous brat. A tropical downpour soaks us on our way across the car park, and I stand on the concourse and bawl like a toddler, in a tantrum about being wet. I am appalled by myself, but cannot help it. I am out of control, and suddenly this feels like the only appropriate way to be; I am not a normal person any more, and have no wish to pretend to all these tourists and airline staff milling around us that I am anything like them.

There is a strange and confronting moment in the smoking lounge. I take a seat at the bar alone, order a drink, and the barmaid studies my face. 'Are you okay?' The room is almost silent; everyone is too busy smoking to chat. 'No,' I say evenly, 'I'm not okay' – and tell her why. She stares. Everyone stares. She comes around the bar and hugs me. A man says to the barmaid, 'Buy her whatever she wants.' I thought people only ever said that in films. Do I like it? I cannot tell.

The airline has made arrangements for us to be escorted onto the plane after everyone else is seated. It is my first intimation of the celebrity of tragedy, and half of me is burning with embarrassment as we take our seats, but the other half almost enjoys making a spectacle of ourselves, and is grateful for the public statement of our difference. Before I fall asleep a steward tells us he read about Tony's death in the papers and can't believe he is now flying us home. I can't tell if I am touched or angry. I hate becoming a freak show – a scrap of anecdote fodder for random strangers – but I also want the special status of our catastrophe to be acknowledged. We have been cocooned in a community where everyone knew what had happened to us, and re-entry to a world which may not know or care is so confusing that I do not know my own mind. When I awake before we come in to land, I stare at the rows of other families returning from their holiday with the father still alive and I think I hate them; I think I feel jealous and bitter. But do I really? Or do I just assume I ought to? I can't be sure. Perhaps I am just making the most of an excuse for ugly misanthropy.

Tom's girlfriend, Shakira, meets us in arrivals at Gatwick and travels back to our house, Tubslake, with us in the taxi. On the way Joe asks me to tell him the story of how Tony died-ed again, so I do. Conscious that the driver and Shakira are listening, mesmerised by the poignancy and close to tears, I sense another intimation of the power of our tragedy – the dangerous appeal of our new specialness – and my uncertainty about the difference between emotional candour and showing off.

My father and his partner, Sarah, are waiting to greet us when we get home. It is a perfect late May day; the garden is a confetti of blossom, and Jake and Joe fall upon their toys in the playroom, soothed with the comfort of familiarity. For eight days I have fixated on getting us home, and now here we are.

But as I walk from room to room I begin to weep. There is no trace of the relief I had anticipated; I don't want to be here at all. I wish we were back in Jamaica. In fact, I would rather be anywhere in the world than here at home.

6

The overwhelming sensation of being home is one of homelessness. That breath of relief as you flop onto your own sofa, whose familiarity I'd always taken for granted, has vanished; I cannot find it anywhere. Even in my own bed there is no sanctuary.

Actually, my bed is the last place to look for it. While we were in Jamaica the builders have transformed the first floor, and our bedroom is barely recognisable from the one Tony and I last slept in. I pace the floorboards, staring up at the beams, absorbing the cold truth that it will never be our bedroom again; it is mine now, 'my bedroom', a phrase so bleakly alien that when I try to say it out loud the words choke me. I haven't slept in 'my' bedroom since my mid-twenties. It feels unnatural, an infantilising regression, like wearing my old school uniform. The boys will never pad along the passage in the morning and climb into their mum and dad's bed again.

Everything has become a metaphor. During supper on our first evening home, Shakira motions to Tom that he has lettuce stuck in his teeth, my father gestures to a bread-crumb on Sarah's cheek, and these two inconsequential moments send me reeling from the room. The world is designed for couples; I no longer fit. Even the most mundane household objects have been stripped of banality and invested with a significance that threatens to capsize me at any moment. Because of the building work, the whole house has been rearranged while we were away, and now I can't find anything, but what should be a series of mild inconveniences – a missing tin opener, central heating I can't operate – become crises, symbolic of a loss of all control.

Being at home is exhausting, but leaving the house is so exposing that I become mildly agoraphobic. Tony's face is on the front page of our local newspaper; his death is announced on billboards along the village high street. 'Local Man Drowns Saving Son'. I find myself cast in a new role I can neither stand nor escape – the public widow – and worry about getting it right.

In the village I sense that people are staring. It is a picturesque and uneventful collection of white weather-board houses and independent stores, but we moved here so recently that I don't yet know any of the shopkeepers. I begin to feel paranoid, trying to work out who does and doesn't know. The teller in the bank seems to be especially gentle, so I think she must know, but then maybe she has always been this lovely? I can't remember. I'm not even sure if I want everyone to know or not. I feel like a liability in public, for at any moment I am in danger of bursting into tears, so a part of me hopes they do. I rather envy the Victorians, because if I were dressed in mourning clothes this problem would be solved, and allowances would presumably be made for any bizarre behaviour.

When I realise I look like a fright, I want to get my eyebrows waxed and do something about my nails, but if I go to the salon in the village will I look unseemly? I picture the beautician in the pub, gossiping with disapproving friends about my shocking sense of priorities, and end up driving to a town miles away, where I can be fairly sure nobody will know me.

I am touched by the postman's condolences when he delivers the mail, and grateful for his kind words. But now each time he has a parcel and has to knock again I feel self-conscious and anxious, because I can't tell how sad I am supposed to look. If I am always in tears, will my grief soon begin to look slovenly and unedifying? Perhaps I am expected to pull myself together – but then I worry that he will think me cold and indifferent.

After a few days Tom's girlfriend Shakira has to go back to London for work. My dad and his partner Sarah need to get back to Wiltshire. But as bags are packed, and motorway routes discussed, panic overtakes me.

When I ask Sarah to stay, my shame at owning up to this new neediness does not surprise me. The only shock is how little I find I care. Dignity can go out the window as long as Sarah doesn't leave, because without her I don't think I am capable of looking after Jake and Joe. So she and Tom stay, my cousin Shona arrives later that week to relieve Sarah, and for the next three months a rota of friends and relatives will occupy the spare room in shifts, so that I am never alone. I'm even helplessly grateful for the company of the builders. Living in a building site is a nightmare, obviously, but I dread the day when they will leave.

The boys go back to nursery, and the rhythm of their old routine seems to stabilise them a little, but their mood swings continue to floor me. Joe keeps asking me to tell him the story about how Tony died-ed again, but every time I begin Jake flies off the handle. Jake doesn't want to talk about it, or even hear Tony's name; he stuffs his fingers in his ears, kicks Joe and bolts out of the room. Frightened that I no longer know how to care for my own children, I go to London with Tom to see Tanya Byron, a child psychologist I know.

I haven't noticed what has happened to my body until we step off the train at Charing Cross into the roar of the capital. Ordinarily I am a typical hurried Londoner, brutally impatient with dawdlers, but now I inch along like a post-operative invalid, getting in everyone's way. Sirens and car horns make me jump and cling to Tom.

In the past, bereaved friends have often described their incredulous fury at the world for continuing to turn, indifferent to their tragedy, and as we walk through Soho I share something of this disbelief. It's not as if I had expected the city to seize up when Tony died; it is just a shock to see that while my world has turned inside out it has been carrying on as normal. An urge to scream 'Haven't you heard?' at passing strangers is also, I understand, quite normal. Given my current state of derangement, that I am not seized by this mad impulse feels like something, at least.

The last time I met Tanya I was interviewing her for the *Guardian*, so it feels strange to present myself as a patient. We meet in the Groucho club. I was here only a month ago, interviewing an author, but now the bearded media types talking loudly about film scripts look like creatures from another planet. We sit outside on the roof terrace and drink coffee. How, I ask Tanya, do I stop Jake blaming himself for Tony's death? Her advice is so breathtakingly simple that I cannot understand how none of us had thought of it.

Everyone has been telling Jake that it was nobody's fault. But to a four-year-old this is worse than meaningless; it is palpably untrue. When something goes wrong, it has to be somebody's fault. Why is everybody lying to him? No wonder we seem to be just making him angrier.

'Tell him it was the sea's fault,' Tanya tells me. And of course, it was. When I say this to Jake the following day, it's as if I have given him a tranquilliser. For the first time since Tony died his body relaxes, and the tension in his eyes eases away.

A few days later we are in the car when I tell the boys something else which has an impact so instant and dramatic that I wonder why it has taken me so long to say. 'I'm so, so sorry,' I tell them. 'I'm so desperately sorry this has happened to you. Everyone is so sorry that this has happened to your family.' It is only when I glance in the rear-view mirror and see the relief on their faces that I realise they have been unsure until now if they are the victims or the cause of all this distress. Ever since Tony died they have been surrounded by grown-ups looking stony-faced, tearful, tense, and have been wondering if they have done something wrong.

Tanya had been less concerned about the boys' state of mind than mine, and it is beginning to dawn on me that I must be in some sort of state of post-traumatic shock. I need to send Ben a simple two-line email, but when I open up the laptop I stare at the screen for three and a half hours, unable to type a single word. Thoughts hurtle about in my head, but I can't seem to convert the mental commotion into any sort of action. In the face of the simplest of tasks, I freeze up in paralysis.

Processing quite basic information is beyond me. I can't concentrate enough to read anything, and don't even contemplate turning on the television. Out of habit I turn on Radio 4, and find it quite soothing, until I discover that I cannot listen to the news. As soon as the pips strike the hour, and I know a bulletin is about to start, my heart begins to race and I am pitched into total panic. News reporters have a special broadcasting voice I had never noticed until now – portentous, urgent, and to my ears now wilfully alarmist. It is a voice that says: I am going to tell you something new and important, and quite possibly shocking. And of course they are; that's their job. But I don't want to hear anything new and important.

After several days I tell myself I am being pathetic. I find a copy of the *Sunday Times* magazine in the living room, and take it to bed to read. The cover story is an article about the Lost Prophets lead singer, Ian Watkins, recently convicted of unimaginable sexual crimes against babies and children. It's the sort of article I have written many times myself. Now I find I am not just unable to read it; I can't even have it in my bedroom. I carry the magazine to the door gingerly, as if it were a dead mouse, and fling it down the stairs, shaking.

I am becoming increasingly preoccupied with amazement at how anyone comes home from fighting in Helmand and is expected to resume normal life. How are refugees fleeing Mogadishu supposed to make a new home in a Tottenham tower block, and fit in with everybody else as if nothing had happened? I watched just one person die, and am left incapable of even making a phone call.

It is a surprise to find myself thinking about how much worse other people's situations are than my own. In the past, whenever I heard others express something similar in the immediate aftermath of their own tragedy I assumed they were probably only saying so to sound like good people. But the sentiment turns out to be quite genuine; tragedy really does expand your circle of empathy.

An even bigger surprise is how I keep forgetting that Tony is dead. It is now more than two weeks since I watched him drown, but I have been too consumed by how he died to comprehend that it means he is dead. Fixated on the horror of what happened, I have failed to grasp what it means; my mind still can't register the permanent reality of its consequence. Each time it hits me that he is actually dead, which it does about once a day, it's as if I am hearing the news for the very first time. I will be filling the dishwasher, or hanging out laundry, when out of the blue the stunning revelation winds me. Tony is *dead*? The perverse amnesia is bewildering. How can I have been thinking about nothing but Tony all the time, and yet keep forgetting?

This cognitive delay may help to explain my peculiar response to correspondence. A mountain of letters and cards is waiting at home when we arrive back from Jamaica, and more keep arriving every day. I am astonished by how much they move me, and feel awful about all the bereaved people I have known and never thought to send a card. I hadn't the faintest idea how much it would mean, and each day's post dissolves me into fresh wonderment at the kindness of the world. But on our first day home, when I open the envelopes my initial reaction is confusion and embarrassment.

I think all these people writing to me have got the wrong end of the stick. They have mistaken my loss for a catastrophe; their letters speak of my family's lifelong pain, they console our devastation. Oh no, I think. How awkward. How has this happened? I appear to have inadvertently tricked them into feeling sorry for me. I feel a total fraud.

When I realise that is not why they have written to me, the shock is chilling. They haven't got the wrong end of the stick at all. They haven't mistaken our situation for something far worse than it is. On the contrary, they are way ahead of me. They understand perfectly. I haven't defrauded them out of sympathy; the only person I have been hoodwinking is myself, in blind denial of the enormity of our loss.

'Dec, do you believe this is really happening?' Tom asks one evening. We are in the kitchen, cooking supper. 'I mean, does it feel real to you? Cos I don't mind telling you, it doesn't to me.' Tom is the most militantly rational person I know. At our C of E primary school, aged ten, he once organised a mass prayer boycott. To hear Tom now confess his own lapse into muddle-headed denial is a huge relief, because with each passing day Tony's death is becoming not more real to me, but less.

In those first hours after he drowned, when the catastrophe was still confined to Calabash beach, and to Jake, Joe and me, its speed was impossible to reconcile with its scale. Nothing so big could happen this fast; it defied the laws of physics, it could not be true. Death is too much for the mind to register in a matter of minutes; the incalculable magnitude can only be absorbed by increment, day by day. As each day allows a new glimpse of its immensity, and the aftershock extends beyond the beach to reach hundreds of people all over the world, my comprehension slowly expands until its dimensions resemble a more accurate impression of the truth. But the bigger his death grows, the more inconceivable it becomes. It feels like an ambitious piece of performance art; a work of fiction, not real life.

How strange that the truth of my own situation should be so much clearer to everybody else. Still, it amazes me that so many people write. Even the staff from our local Tesco send a card. What is it about a death like Tony's that can hold such power over our collective imagination? Had he died of cancer I wouldn't receive cards from people I barely know. It is sudden death that galvanises our emotions. But if Tony had died suddenly of a stroke I still don't think old school friends I have not seen for twenty years would get in touch. It must have something to do with the horror of tragedy's proximity to innocent pleasure which we find so haunting, for we can all picture ourselves on holiday with our family. The possibility that one of us might not come home seems to evoke the primitive terror of a folk tale.

In a filing cabinet in my father's study is a folder full of the letters and cards he received when my mum died. As a child I used to find them comforting to read, even though most were from people I didn't even know. So I buy a big box to store all the correspondence that keeps arriving, and ask a colleague at the *Guardian* to send us all the newspaper reports of Tony's death, for the boys to read when they are older. As I'm boxing everything up, I'm struck by a thought so dangerously ugly, I want to scrub my brain with bleach.

I see there's been no card or letter from X, whispers a toxic voice in my head. Nope, nor anything from Y.

Christ, what is wrong with me? Is this what grief will do

to me; does sadness curdle into monstrous self-importance? Horrified by myself, I become hyper-alert for any new warning signs of narcissistic entitlement.

When I was pregnant with Jake, I used to wonder whether motherhood was going to change me. Everybody said it would. I didn't much like the sound of the new emotional landscape reported by friends with new babies, and couldn't fathom why they all seemed so relaxed about turning into uptight neurotics. Who would want to be in a constant state of anxiety over disasters that are never going to happen, endlessly fretting about colic and faulty travel cots and whether the next-door neighbour is a paedophile? 'Do you know,' one old friend actually boasted, 'before Alex was born I used to feel quite compassionate towards paedophiles. Now whenever I think about them I feel *murderous*.'

When none of this came to pass in my case, I wasn't just relieved. Although I did not like to admit it to anyone, I was also a tiny bit smug. Jake was always a strikingly fearless child, and privately I credited his confidence to my unwillingness to subscribe to this perverse parental cult of fearfulness. But one evening as I am putting the boys to bed, I see Jake's face darken. This is happening a lot; he's fine one minute, and then a grey cloud settles across his features and he disappears inside himself.

'What's wrong, Jake?' I ask. 'I'm frightened,' he says. 'What are you frightened of?' He considers the question for a while. 'I'm just frightened,' he says eventually. And I realise that is exactly what I am now, too. I'm not frightened of anything in particular. I am frightened of everything, and more specifically of everyone.

Sometimes I used to wonder why I have always been drawn to people whose appeal is not conventionally obvious, when it would probably be wiser to spend one's life around straightforwardly sensible friends. But the company of those who are not terribly stable or considered can be terrific fun, if they can't hurt you. And nobody ever could. I could absorb almost limitless amounts of other people's idiocy without ever feeling upset, because to me it was only ever fascinating. I was surprised everyone else didn't see life the same way. Why let yourself feel offended or wounded, when you could be interested and amused instead?

Now almost anyone can undo me. They don't even have to try. The day after we get home from Jamaica a man from our local village knocks on the door to offer his condolences. He was a friend of Tony's, and means well, but everything he says is horribly wrong. It ranges from the glib ('Oh well, we're all going to die, that's just life') to the staggeringly self-regarding ('I mean, it may be my turn next, have you thought of that?') to the pseudo-mystical ('You do know he hasn't died, don't you? He's still here, he's just changed shape'). It is a five-star tour de force of what not to say, and within minutes I have to mumble some sort of excuse and flee upstairs to hide in my bed, trembling, barely able to breathe. If all it takes is some well-meant crassness to take me apart, the world is suddenly a terrifying place.

It was because nothing ever used to make me feel afraid that I never thought of Tony as my protector. In the beginning this had been surprisingly problematic. Old-school manliness had been so central to his self-image that a new relationship which rendered it redundant quite unnerved him. If that wasn't his role, then who else was he expected to be? And why was I even interested in him? To Tony it made no sense.

In my experience, men who make a meal of their masculinity do so chiefly because they have little else to offer. I only began to grasp how much more there was to Tony when he accommodated himself to this conundrum of my stated independence, and made himself indispensable in all sorts of new and unfamiliar ways which did not involve threatening to beat anyone up. But that was only part of the story, I see now. I was too bowled over by Tony's capacity for what Americans would call 'personal growth' to notice that I, too, was changing – although in my case the shift was less impressive.

The invulnerability so central to my own self-image turns out to have been a self-delusion; a necessary invention. A couples therapist I know once told me that the qualities we look for in a partner are those we needed as a child and were denied – and so of course, Tony's protection had appealed to something deeply hidden within me. After all these years together, I have grown accustomed to depending on him to protect me, and hadn't even noticed. Now, without him, I discover I am afraid of everything – burglars, Vladimir Putin, gypsies, jihadis, the future – and the literalism of my nightmares is almost embarrassing, like a schoolgirl's idea of the unconscious.

In one recurring dream, I come out of a shop in Maidstone to see a gang of lads break into Tony's car and speed away. I go home to wait for them. How I know they will be driving to our house is lost in the illogic of the dream; all I know is that any minute now they are about to drive through the gate. I stand at the upstairs bathroom window, watching, waiting. When Tony's car pulls in, the doors swing open and a band of cartoon hoodlums pour out and swagger towards our front door.

I turn from the window, and standing right in front of me is Tony. I am dissolved with relief: I am euphoric. He gathers me into his arms, and together we watch from the landing as the men burst into the hallway below. They have axes and hammers, and set about swinging them at walls and doors, cackling wildly as they smash up the house. I couldn't be less scared. Everything is alright, because Tony has come back to take care of me, and those goons down there have no idea what's about to hit them. I almost laugh at the first one to bound up the stairs towards us – until he walks right through Tony. The vandals do not even see him. He is just a ghost, visible only to me.

I was brought up to regard even the mildest anxiety about personal security as ideologically suspect and vaguely shaming. I didn't own a key until I left home, and as far as I know my father's house has no locks to this day. Until I got to university, I didn't know you were supposed to remove the car key from the ignition. Trust in the world was an article of faith for my family, and when my dad's car was stolen from outside the house a few years ago he could not have been more astonished if it had been abducted by aliens.

Part of me can of course now see the machismo of our contempt for safety concerns. It is equally clear to me that I am now a single woman living with two small children in the countryside. Were someone to break into Tubslake in the middle of the night, what exactly would I be able to do about it? Under these new circumstances, my old snootiness about security is a self-indulgent posture, and plainly irresponsible. But none of this makes my call to the electrician any easier. Asking for a burglar alarm to be installed feels awkward, but just about bearable. Asking for a panic button in my bedroom is more of a challenge, and becomes a confusing conversation for the poor electrician, because I literally cannot bring myself to say the words.

I am finding it impossible to believe that Tony does not know he is dead. How can he not know? In my mind he is watching us, and apart from the new alarm system, of which he would wholeheartedly approve, everything I do feels treacherous. When I interview a woman as a potential future nanny for the boys when I go back to work, I have to maintain a performance of sanity for her. It is a beautiful summer day, so I carry a tray of coffee and biscuits out into the garden and we sit in the sunshine, watching the boys play on the fireman's pole the builders have built for them, and I try to sound like a plausible employer. We talk about nursery pickup times and hourly rates, but all

I am thinking is, how must this look to Tony? What am I doing, inviting a stranger into his home to look after his children?

Of all the startling revelations these first weeks bring, one shakes me perhaps more than any other. Some experiences, I am discovering, really are too painful to talk about. It is becoming clear to me that the story of how Tony died is what everybody wants to hear, and even when they don't say so I sense them waiting, angling, hoping it will come. Being immensely nosey and often quite prurient myself, I know I would be exactly like that too, so I am not at all offended by their curiosity. It is just that I don't have the strength to keep satisfying it. I am amazed by what it costs me each time I have to tell the story, and see for the first time why others have been unable to talk about trauma in their life.

But I see, too, that how Tony died is currency. Most of the time I can choose not to spend it, but every now and then, when someone is especially kind or generous, I feel obliged under the terms of some bizarre contractual barter to offer them the story in return.

This is not, it turns out, the only form of currency he left behind. In Jamaica Matt had asked if I was afraid of what I might find out about Tony. 'Are you worried you might discover any secrets?' It took a moment to understand what he meant. But of course, one of the clichés of a sudden death is the posthumous discovery of a double life – a hidden mistress, a massive gambling debt, even a secret second family. Tony often had the manner of a man who might well be keeping something under his hat, so I could see why Matt would ask, but his question made me laugh. 'No, Matty, I can safely say that's about the only thing in the world I'm not remotely worried about right now.'

We were still in Jamaica when I received a text from our builder, an unflappable Czech called Bago who the boys have renamed Bagpuss. His texts are normally economical two-liners, but this one ran to four paragraphs, and began: 'There is an issue.' My father was arriving at the house the following day, and Bago wanted to know what to do about 'Tony's plants in the barn'. Should he get rid of them, or did I have other plans for them?

I couldn't think what he was talking about. Then I remembered. Of course. Months earlier, Tony had mentioned that he was going to grow a couple of cannabis plants in one of the barns. I had been doubtful about the plan, but there was no talking him out of it. 'Oh Dec, half the county grow their own. It's a piece of cake.' What if he got caught? 'Well, for a start, I won't. And even if I did, Old Bill don't nick you for a few plants. It counts as personal.'

In the event, it seemed to me to be more bother than it was worth. Tony was forever faffing about with plant food and disappearing off to the barn to check on acidity levels or something. I left him to it. After an inordinate palaver he harvested a disappointing crop of mediocre weed, and although he claimed to have worked out where he had gone wrong, and was sure the next crop would be a winner, I suspected this was the end of his horticultural experiment.

We would be leaving for Jamaica in a few weeks anyway, so a second go at it would obviously have to wait, and I guessed the holiday gave Tony a good excuse to suspend operations without losing face.

Bago must have found the growing equipment in the barn. I had never even been in there to take a look, but imagined there must be a light or two, and perhaps a fan. If my dad came across it he would have no idea what it was, and wouldn't care less even if he did. I texted Bago back telling him not to worry.

We have been home for a fortnight when Bago makes a joke about 'the farm'. What does he mean? He looks at me in surprise. 'You know, the *farm*.' What farm? 'Follow me,' Bago says. He leads me out to the barn, through the gloom to the back, where I find a gigantic canvas tent. He unzips one corner, and I take a step back.

It is not a couple of plants; it's a modestly sized cannabis factory. There are industrial-strength fans, blinding lights, a complicated-looking automated irrigation system, and those stainless steel ventilation flues you see outside kebab shops – and in the middle of it all, a small forest of bushy cannabis plants, practically as tall as me. Whoever Tony recruited to feed them while we were away has done a first-rate job. Though not exactly the sort of surprise Matt was worried about, it is so perfectly Tony that I laugh until I cry.

We zip the tent back up and I go and find Tom to ask what we do now. 'Well hats off to Tone,' he agrees, after taking a look in the barn. It would have looked, to anyone who didn't know Tony, like a commercial operation. But so prodigious was his personal consumption of cannabis the entire contents of the barn would only have been enough to keep him going. In the face of my objections to the cost of his smoking so much, his solution had been not to smoke less, but to grow it all instead. How much would the crop be worth if we kept it going until harvest time? We try to speculate, but keep getting the giggles and give up.

This is probably not the time, we reluctantly agree, for a *Breaking Bad* adventure, so I phone one of Tony's friends in London who knows about these things, and ask him to come and dismantle everything and take it away. I would make an unpromising cannabis farmer under the best of circumstances. To launch a criminal career would be a particularly tall order when we have a funeral to organise.

7

If you believe in God, it can't be all that hard to organise a funeral. The religious service observes rituals so long established that no one even notices the format unless something goes badly wrong. A secular funeral, on the other hand, is more complicated, and quite like mufti day at school. Once you dispense with traditional uniformity, you forfeit its power to protect you, and expose yourself to all sorts of scrutiny and judgement. Every choice, every detail, becomes a personalised statement of identity. When Tom volunteers for the job of organising Tony's funeral, neither he nor I have begun to grasp what a minefield of taste and politics, race and class we will have to navigate.

The easy part is ruling out all the things we don't want.

I am not a fan, for example, of the rococo horse-drawn glass coffin, the ostentatiously elongated funeral car procession, the over-styled outfits that look like fancy dress, or any of the other showy bling of a contemporary east London funeral. Tom can't stand the sentimental prohibition of 'speaking ill of the dead', which manifests as an injunction against anyone saying anything remotely meaningful or even true about the person they are burying. The curious convention of excluding young children, even when it is their own parent being buried, has always baffled both of us.

On the other hand, I have almost no idea what I actually do want. I love organising parties; I am really good at it. But I have never organised a funeral before, nor given a moment's thought to how one might go about it.

Tom moves in with us for a month, and we become full-time events organisers – only without the unflappable calm I imagine the job usually involves. To invent a ceremony that will do Tony justice while so dysfunctional with grief that I still cannot make a phone call feels both impossible and imperative, and a degree of mania quickly sets in. There is no mobile-phone signal inside the house, so Tom sits in the garden all day, soldered to his iPhone, endlessly drawing up and revising lists. 'Tom's favourite game,' Jake says when he gets home from nursery one day, 'is sitting on a rock by the pond, talking to his phone.' He is managing upwards of 200 calls a day, and developing the robotic glaze of a call-centre worker; I take him out a cup of tea one day, and overhear him actually haggling with the gravedigger.

(To be fair, grave digging turns out to be pricier than you might think. For reasons no one can explain, if we want a Saturday burial – which we do – we will have to pay double the going rate, which comes to £400. A career switch from record producer to gravedigger is an option Tom had not previously considered, but given the parlous state of today's music industry we both agree it's one worth bearing in mind.)

Every night, after the boys are in bed, we sit at the kitchen table and agonise over each of the day's decisions, then go to bed and start all over again the next morning. We are making it up as we go along. The only thing this feels remotely like is the memory of organising our weddings.

As with a wedding, the first thing to find is the venue. The Roundchapel is an imposingly graceful Victorian former church just a few hundred yards from our old house in Hackney; the bar next door belongs to a good friend of Tony's, who agrees to host the wake, where Tom's ex-girlfriend, the DJ Smokin' Jo, will play. A cut-and-paste eulogy by a stranger who never even met the deceased is another funeral convention I have never understood, so instead several of Tony's friends, and his daughter, will talk about his life. I want to speak, too, but quickly realise this will be a problem.

I have always been surprised and mildly embarrassed by my enthusiasm for public speaking. I don't enjoy appearing on TV, have never wanted to act, and the very thought of karaoke brings me out in a cold sweat. But oddly, when it comes to public speaking I have no inhibitions. The first audience I have ever felt incapable of addressing turns out to be Tony's congregation – I don't know why; I just know that I can't – so I ask a friend to read words I can write but cannot read.

I had assumed the writing part would be easy, until I sit down and try. My advice to the other speakers was simple: just tell the truth and be yourself, but now I see this was easier to offer than to follow. I do not want to be sentimental, and I don't want to lie, but I don't want to offend anyone or put my foot in it either, which leaves surprisingly little narrative room to manoeuvre.

There is something else I also need to write. What people want and need, more than anything, is an explanation. Most don't like to phone me, and the few that do get no answer, so they call Tom instead, and the question everyone keeps asking him is: how did Tony drown? It was reported in detail by every national newspaper, and it is rather confronting to learn that Fleet Street's broadly accurate account was assumed by almost everyone to be a lie.

I'm not sure I will survive if I have to spend all afternoon at the Roundchapel retelling the story of his death. So instead I draft an account to be inserted into the order of service, with a note to say that we hope it will spare the need for anyone to ask me to explain how he died on the day. I worry that it will look like a passive-aggressive rebuke to perfectly valid curiosity, and feel queasy about writing about myself in the third person, but when I show it to Tom the only change he suggests is one that I hadn't even thought of. 'People keep asking me if he was drunk. So instead of saying he went down to the beach in the morning, be more specific – you need to say it was around eight-thirty a.m.'

The list of decisions to be made never seems to get any shorter or easier. Words are my department, but music is Tom's, and every night we trawl my iPod in search of inspiration. I would like to play the Rihanna song 'Stay', but Tom correctly points out that it would sound tacky. Does that matter? Yes, I realise, it does. We don't want hymns, but we do want their gravitas. In the end the only secular music we can find that feels dignified, unifying and authentically evocative of Tony is vintage reggae, and it is a happy surprise when we listen to 'One Love' by Bob Marley and realise it sounds just like a hymn.

Giles Fraser comes to see us in Kent. Giles used to be canon of St Paul's cathedral, until he resigned in solidarity with the Occupy movement and became, in his words, 'the *Guardian*'s pet vicar'. He has offered to officiate, so we sit in my garden and discuss the service, smoking and swearing excessively. I am relieved he doesn't mind my prohibition on any mention of God, and mildly ashamed at my pride in his approval of our plans. I worry that I am turning Tony's funeral into a public performance – but feel better when Giles explains why he has no worries about our secular format. It's only when wankers die, he says, that you need scripture and ritual to fall back on.

When every detail of the service and wake has been

decided, we are still only halfway there. Even if we have got everything right, and Tony's funeral evokes some of his truth for all the people coming, there will be two for whom it will be almost meaningless. To Jake and Joe it will at best be just a load of grown-ups talking – and at worst an overwhelming crowd of strangers who Jake worries are angry with him for causing Tony's death.

And so, after long deliberation, we come up with what I naïvely imagine to be a solution. We will bury Tony the following day, at a small country cemetery a few miles from our home, and invite only the people who are most important to the boys. There will be no formal ceremony at the graveside, because more words can mean nothing to them now. Instead we will sing 'Amazing Grace'. I have to teach the words to Jake and Joe, and we rehearse in the car on the morning drive to nursery. Joe likes it and is keen to sing, but most days Jake refuses to join in. 'I hate that song,' he says angrily, and stares out the window.

During the month we spend organising the funeral, there are other, more unexpected challenges that vary from the comic to the macabre. Uncertainty about the appropriate dress code is generating so much anxiety, Tom soon reports, that he thinks we will have to specify one in the invitation. I think that would look mad; this isn't a cocktail party. But it is a problem. In my family, you do not wear black to a funeral, and in Tony's world you categorically do. I don't want to confuse or offend anyone, but I don't want to feel like a fraud either. I just want people to wear whatever they feel comfortable in. But no matter how many times Tom tells everyone this, they won't stop calling for clarification. I am amazed clothes could matter so much. But I lose my nerve about the multicoloured dress I had planned to wear, and opt for black instead.

I hadn't anticipated that organising a funeral would involve negotiating with HMP Belmarsh, until one of Tony's colleagues gets in touch with a new problem. On his very first day at Kids Company Tony had been assigned a young man I will call Richard. Of all the youngsters Tony worked with, none drove him madder or tested his patience more severely. But he was the one Tony loved more deeply than any other, and if the principle behind Kids Company was surrogate parenting then in this case it was truly realised. Tony was the closest thing Richard has ever known to a real father. After yet another aborted apprenticeship, at a loss for what to try next Tony once brought Richard home and taught him to cook in our kitchen. I have been worrying about how Richard will have taken the news of Tony's death, and know how frantic he must be to attend the funeral. The trouble is, he is currently on remand in Belmarsh for murder.

What would be the appropriate tone for an email to the governor of Belmarsh? If such a thing exists then I fail to strike it, because nothing I come up with cuts any ice. 'Unless the deceased is next of kin,' she replies, 'we do not facilitate attendance at funerals.' I know Tony would not have given up this easily, but can't think what else to do – until I remember the Lib Dem MP Sarah Teather. She had emailed her condolences while we were in Jamaica, and like everyone else said if there was anything she could do then I must just ask. I can't imagine she was thinking of anything along these lines, but after a quick Google establishes that there are Lib Dem ministers in the department for justice, I ask if she can persuade them to change the governor's mind. I remember a former Tory prisons minister we met at Jake's two years earlier, and although the connection is tenuous to say the least, I rattle off an email to him too.

Both politicians do everything they can, as does my local MP. I don't even know who he is until I consult Google, and discover to my mortification that we now live in the constituency of Tunbridge Wells – not an eventuality my younger Hackney self could have predicted, nor a state of affairs I imagine will do me any favours when what I need is a politician willing to lobby for compassion on behalf of a south London murder suspect. The MP for Tunbridge Wells turns out to be a Tory minister who confounds all my prejudices. His efforts to talk the governor round are heroic, and though ultimately fruitless – Richard will not be allowed to attend – make me feel bad about slagging off Tories all the time.*

I get the impression that the governor's intransigence comes as a relief to one or two people. Would I really, they venture tentatively, have wanted a prisoner in handcuffs under guard in the front row? Actually, yes, I would. For all I care, Richard could have come in an orange jumpsuit and

---

* Richard stood trial and was found not guilty the following year.

shackles as long as he got the chance to say his goodbye, and I think Tony would have thoroughly enjoyed inconveniencing the prison service. Besides, it wouldn't even have been the most bizarre element of Tony's funeral. Not by a long way. That distinction would have to go to a local shopkeeper who tries to extort money out of me.

I send out an invitation to the funeral by group text from Tony's phone, to every name I can identify in his contacts. This requires a fair bit of detective work, on account of his dyslexia and his friends' obscurely tangential nicknames – Greeny Dani, Martin one whe, Iron Dresd, etc. When the group text has finally gone out, a reply pings in minutes later from this man I shall call W. 'Hi mate any chance of that money u owe me please.'

What? I'm completely thrown. I call him on Tony's phone. W answers straight away.

'Alright mate, how you doing?'

'Sorry, this isn't Tony. It's Decca.'

'Oh.' He sounds surprised. 'Why, what's up with Tone then?'

'Have you not heard the news? Tony is dead. He died three weeks ago.'

I hear him gasp. 'Look if Tony owed you some money, of course I'll sort you out,' I go on. 'But did you not just receive an invitation to his funeral?' If it didn't reach W, how will I know who else it didn't reach? 'What text?' He sounds bemused. So I send him the invitation again, and a few minutes later W texts back. 'Just got that it was 600 he owed me I am so sorry to here that he was a good friend

I will try and make it if there is anything I can do just text me x'

Tony hardly knew this man. They only met a few months ago; he has never even been to our house. How could Tony possibly owe him £600? For that matter, why would W lend a man he barely knows that much money? But who would make such a thing up? Another text arrives from W: 'Sorry 4 having to ask 4 the money it's a shock.' I have to go and collect the boys from nursery, but am so dazed by this exchange that I get into my pickup and don't even see Tony's car until I smash straight into it.

Tom and I spend the next three days painstakingly re-texting Tony's friends one by one, asking them to confirm receipt of the invite. It appears that everyone got it. But W texts Tony's phone again, asking me for the money. Although over six foot, Tom isn't particularly big, but he can be quite intimidating when he wants to, and one afternoon he goes to pay W a visit in his shop while I wait outside.

Tom emerges after a few minutes, and climbs back into the passenger seat. 'The man's a pathetic little prick,' he spits. 'As soon as I started shouting at him, the little prick goes to pieces. All he could say was, "I'm so sorry, sir, I'm so sorry, sir, it was just the shock. I was just so shocked to hear about Tony, I didn't know what I was doing." Forget about him, Dec, he's just a twat.'

But a week later, the roofer who rents one of our barns happens to tell me about the morning he read of Tony's death in his *Sunday Mirror*. 'I couldn't believe my eyes.

Didn't know what to do. I just got on the phone and started ringing everyone I could think of who knew him. The first one I called was W.' W? Is he sure? The roofer looks puzzled. 'Course I'm sure. I remember it like it was yesterday.' Tony knew some exceptionally unpleasant people in his criminal career, but I doubt any of them would be capable of something as dark as pretending not to know he was dead in order to rip off his widow for a few hundred quid.

W can at least be disinvited to the funeral. Our bigger problem is a relative of Tony's who will not stop phoning Tom, hysterical and belligerent. Nothing Tom can say satisfies her need for acknowledgement of her own loss. When she threatens to turn up and force her way into the house, 'to look after Decca and the boys', he tells her he will lock the door and phone the police. So instead she starts emailing Tony.

The emails are truly disturbing. They open with 'How are you?' and sign off 'Speak soon.' I don't know what else to do but ignore them, until one arrives demanding – no, insisting – she be allowed to speak at the funeral. I am aghast. I have always been fond of her, but am desperate to protect Tony's dignity, and in her current state I am terrified of what she might say. But I do not think I have the moral authority to refuse her.

Tony's daughter does, and fires off a fairly robust email, telling her to stop sending weird emails and forget about making a speech. But now I worry that this relative may have a go at her at the funeral. It would probably only take a dirty look to provoke Tony's daughter, and if that happens her mother might well wade in too. I would guess that security is not a standard fixture on the funeral checklist, and am joking when I suggest it might be wise to hire a bouncer. But the prospect of a cat fight breaking out between Tony's relative, his ex-wife and his daughter at his own funeral is so unconscionably awful that Tom books a female bouncer just in case.

As each decision is made, the narcotic allure of agency begins to ring alarm bells. Having always been prone to fantasies of omnipotence, I am familiar with the delusion that making plans means taking control, and can see how easily I might absorb myself in all these details to distract from the unbearable reality of helplessness. Is that what Tom and I are really doing, as we obsess and fret over the minutiae of the funeral? But no, it isn't that. Until you have to organise one yourself, it is impossible to appreciate the enormity of the responsibility. To honour another human being's life is a terrifying undertaking, and the imperative to get it right consumes me. And yet, at the same time, I couldn't care less.

Because what does it matter if we get this or that detail right? It won't change anything. The most dazzlingly brilliant ceremony in the world won't bring Tony back, so who cares if the food is West Indian or Persian, or whether the Roundchapel's piano has been tuned? When it's all over, he will still be dead.

I am not even clear who this funeral is meant to be for. Not me, that much at least I know. Given the choice I would rather not even go, and although this option is plainly out of the question I am under no illusion that the day will hold any emotional value for me. From the furtively studied nonchalance of the boys' occasional questions, I can tell Jake and Joe are not looking forward to it. The only person whose approval I find myself constantly consulting is Tony's. But he is the one person who definitely will not be there, so who are we doing it for? There are moments when I wonder if I must be quite mad to care so much about creating an event I wish to God was not happening, and do not even want to attend.

Someone else who will not be there fills my thoughts. As the day draws near I become obsessively preoccupied by Tony's birth mother. In the past I had only ever pictured her as the underage teenager who gave him up for adoption, but now I cannot stop thinking about the middle-aged woman who must have wondered about her son every day for nearly fifty years – and will still be wondering. The image of her in my mind torments me. She deserves to know her son is dead. But of course, I do not know how to find her.

On the morning of the funeral, I wake up beside Jake and Joe in a hotel bed in Hackney. The outfits they have chosen are neatly folded on a chair; Jake wants to wear his green Usain Bolt T-shirt and yellow shorts, Joe his pink T-shirt from Jake's hotel, and bright pink shorts. It is what they wore most days in Jamaica, and as I get them dressed I am braced for the pathos of their choices to undo me. But I feel nothing. Even as we walk hand in hand through Hackney to the Roundchapel, across the parks where Tony and I used to play with them, past the pubs we used to drink in and the restaurants he loved, I feel nothing at all – literally nothing.

Having dreaded the agony of this day for so long I am thrown by this icy blank numbness, and mildly appalled. What is wrong with me? I am leading my sons to their father's funeral, and even when I try to make myself feel something – anything – I cannot feel a thing. The hearse carrying Tony's coffin is parked outside the Roundchapel when we arrive, and for a fleeting second shocks me out of my anaesthesia. But as I register the gathering crowd of mourners, I sense myself disappear again. I can see it is, by anyone's standards, a wildly incongruous congregation. There are three or four hundred people here – *Guardian* journalists, Kids Company teenagers, East End villains, Kentish farmers, mums and dads from Jake and Joe's nursery. But in my dissociated confusion, and this sea of black clothing, I struggle to recognise faces. Even close friends are hard to place, and I have to bluff my way hopefully through hugs and greetings.

The service passes in a daze. As far as I can tell, everything seems to go to plan. What had never occurred to me during all the endless preparations was that the mourners would want to talk to me. How could I have overlooked something so obvious? I am completely unprepared for any obligation to make appropriate conversation, and to this day can barely recall a word anyone said. Among the afternoon's many surreal exchanges is a moment when I'm belatedly realising that the man I am hugging is Alastair

Campbell when a woman taps me on the shoulder and introduces herself as Tony's therapist.

By the evening I have nothing left in me, and we retreat to my friend's house with close relatives and friends. Tom goes off to the bar, and returns with reports of raucously hedonistic chaos. I am delighted, because it is exactly what Tony would have wanted, and also immensely relieved not to be there.

The following morning a minibus takes some of us home to Kent, while others follow in cars. It is a blazing midsummer day by the time three dozen of us assemble at the cemetery. The previous day's numbness has vanished, and the scene is in blinding technicolour. While we wait for Tony in the sunshine, an undertaker teaches Jake how to pull the bell rope in the tiny chapel, and so when the hearse carrying Tony pulls in through the gates the bell rings out to greet him. The undertakers show my three brothers, my father, my cousin and one of Tony's friends how to carry the coffin to the grave. Joe wants to help, so I hoist him onto my hip and he holds the foot of the coffin as we inch our way unsteadily forward.

We had still been in Jamaica when Jenni had suggested we should fill the grave ourselves. She said it would be profoundly moving. I had wondered why. What difference would it make? And wouldn't it take for ever? It is not until three of us take spades and begin shovelling earth that I see what she meant. In the midsummer heat sweat streams with the tears down our cheeks as spades pass from hand to hand. No one says a word; the only sound is the scrunch of the shovels and the thud of falling earth. When each one of us has helped fill the grave, the primitive symbolism takes our breath away. It doesn't feel like we are burying Tony, so much as tucking him in. Jake and Joe plant violets in the mound.

I had not thought myself susceptible to a pseudo-spiritual preoccupation with 'the body'. To my mind, a corpse was just what is left after somebody dies. So the intensity of my relief that Tony is now no longer in the custody of strangers, but safely buried close to home, astounds me. But this surprise is as nothing to what comes nine days later.

On the day of the funeral service I didn't cross paths with one of Tony's oldest friends, but had thought nothing of it at the time. When I receive a voicemail from him a week later, asking me to call, I can't get through or leave a message, so send the following text:

'I've tried calling but it says phone's unavailable, hope you get this, I'm so sorry we didn't get to speak at t's funeral, your family was such a lovely strength and presence, I really hope you felt happy about how it went, and I hope we see each other soon xxxxxxxxxx'

I think his reply is a joke at first. As I read on, my eyes widen.

'To be honest I was really disappointed. The service and church reception went well but it wasn't about all that. As a black man it is important to bury your people and put the dirt on your loved ones if you can. That's like personally closing the door on their life with your blessing. We wasn't allowed to do that. I've known Tony for 25 years. He's dead and buried but most of his REAL friends weren't privelege to bury fallen brethren. I won't speak for others but I'm really hurt and offended by the decision makers decisions. I don't feel Tony got the burial he deserved, surrounded by people that made and named him TONY DREAD. Another shameful and disrespected thing about all of this, the wreath saying TONY DREAD was left behind at the church. What the fuck!!! I thank you for helping to turn Tonys life around and giving I'm two beautiful children. However I feel you, and or whoever else, let him down when it was obvious what he would have wanted'

As I reread the text, over and over, I know it should outrage me. Instead it quite dismantles me. I feel septic, poisoned by the words and my horror that Tony's burial has been contaminated by anger. All I can think or care about is how to detoxify it. So I write an email apologising for causing offence and explaining that the private burial was for Jake and Joe. I say how sorry I am for having not thought to explain this sooner, and how sorry I am that the wreath was left behind. I tell them it had been delivered to the grave two days later, as soon as I was made aware of it. I apologise again and again.

Not one replies. But I think I understand how a funeral can become a battleground over ownership of the deceased, because it can be easier for the bereaved to find something to be angry about than to let themselves feel sad. I recognise this, because protecting myself from sadness is what I have been doing for pretty much most of my life.

I am forty-three years old, and haven't the first clue about how to grieve. I am an expert in grief-avoidance. In fact, I strongly suspect that had Tony survived long enough to get to hospital, just twenty-four hours on a life-support machine would have bought me enough time to decide not to mind very much when he died. But Tony's death happened too quickly for my normal defences to organise themselves, and so for the first time I am at the mercy of grief. Ever since I turned ten, nobody's death had meant anything to me – because once you have decided you don't mind your own mum dying, how could anyone else's death bother you?

8

Some memories resemble photographs, and others are more like video clips; snatches of an old life that freeze as abruptly as they begin. I have one of Tom and me at home, when I am nine and he's eleven. I am following him from one room to the next, and as we reach the doorway I say something that makes him turn around. I'm astonished to see that he is crying. What's the matter with him? Tom's face is all red and choked up with snot and tears. 'What do you think's the fucking matter?' he shouts at me. 'I'm upset because my mum's fucking dying!' He shoves ahead, and I stare after him, completely bewildered. He's crying because of *that*?

It is one of the most precise memories I have left of the year when our mother was dying. In December 1979 she was diagnosed with terminal lung cancer, and gathered us together to tell us that the doctors thought she had perhaps twelve months left to live. She sat on the sofa beneath the window in the living room, with her legs curled underneath her, leaning against our father's arm. She was thirty-seven; he was thirty-nine.

My brothers were ten, twelve and fourteen, and I was eight. I don't know if we cried, but I am fairly sure she didn't. I can't remember what anyone said. When I was older I used to wonder why Tom's outburst months later had soldered itself on my memory, when so much of that year had drifted from view. It seems obvious to me now. His rage was as unforgettable as seeing an adult steal, shocking because it was a transgression.

It's not possible for me to know if we used to be a happy family. Everyone tells me we were, but the extravagance of bliss they recall cannot be wholly reliable, for tragedy plays havoc with truth. Disaster tends to cast an unreal light of perfection over what came before. But we were probably happy, or happy enough, and certainly looked so.

We lived in a hamlet of half a dozen eighteenth-century houses called Long Dean, at the foot of a narrow, wooded valley. Later than Laurie Lee, but long before rural gentrification, it was a version of childhood closer to *Cider with Rosie* than the manicured formality I find when I go back today. The four of us went ferreting, fished in the river, built treehouses in the woods, kept a goat and a crow for pets. The nearest town was miles away, and consumerism several years off; in old photographs we look like raggle-taggle gypsies, wild in a patchwork of jumble-sale jeans. When old friends of our parents came to visit from London, I would sometimes catch the breath of their wistful longing – a kind of dreamy enchantment with our life.

Our mother's death began so innocently, it didn't cross my mind to be scared. Our doctor's surgery in those days was a room in his private home. He lived in a honey-coloured village a mile up the valley, in a house overlooking a fourteenth-century market cross. The doctor was a tall man, angular and lean; had he not been a family friend, I might have found him quite forbidding. But his house held no fears for my six-year-old self, the day we went to see him about a lump in my mother's breast.

She used to wear soft, practical bras. They might have been Playtex Cross Your Heart bras, and were always off-white from the wash, with straps wide enough for three hook-and-eye fasteners at the back. I sat in a corner and watched my mother undress to the waist. Our family was relaxed about nudity – I didn't know you could be anything else – and I sensed no atmosphere in the room. 'A lump in my breast.' It sounded innocent, like a lump in your pocket, more a child's word than a medical term.

When she had to go for tests to determine whether the lump was cancerous, she explained to us the probabilities. Only one in ten lumps ever turned out to be malignant. They would almost certainly find it was benign. I'd never heard these words before, but something in the sound of one had communicated itself already. Be-nign sounded relatively neutral; it could mean almost anything. Mal-ig-nant could only be bad.

The hospital was in Bath, and this was vaguely un-settling, for though only 12 miles away, Bath was reserved for shopping expeditions, which happened only once or twice a year. But the odds were simple to understand – just one out of every ten – and the way she articulated them seemed to eliminate even this tiny mathematical chance. I had never heard of cancer before, or known anyone to be ill, so had no reason to doubt the equilibrium with which our mother appeared to regard the whole affair.

When she had to tell us that her breast was going to be removed, I still don't remember a great deal of drama. It was the necessary, sensible solution to the problem of this lump. The language of fear or disfigurement never featured in family conversations, and so it never entered my head. When we visited her after the operation, four fuzzy brown and blonde heads around the hospital bed, I only remem-ber her smiling.

It must have been summer, because we packed up the VW van as usual and set off to Scotland for the annual holiday on my grandparents' farm. She stayed behind for the first week, to convalesce – another unfamiliar word – before joining us. We were playing near the byre on our grandparents' farm when we heard the car pull up, and I can remember running across the gravel towards her. She was carrying a brown paper bag with something round inside it, and I asked if it was her old breast. She crouched down to hug me. 'No,' she laughed, 'I've brought you peaches,' and she handed me one.

As far as I could tell, having one breast was almost the same as having two. The main difference was that she had to wear a special bra, with one normal cup and one filled with something soft and spongy. She would let me play with it, and the feel of it made me laugh. But she looked just the same when she had her clothes on, and seemed un-selfconscious about the thick red scar when she undressed. She would swim naked with us in the river at Long Dean, and I thought nothing of it.

On Saturday mornings we used to go to the swimming baths in the local town, and I was startled when she used a cubicle to change. By then I had discovered that some people didn't like to be seen without their clothes on, and must have grasped our family's subtle moral distinction between those who hid away in cubicles, and people like us who got changed in the open. What was she doing in a cubicle? I was embarrassed. 'Oh,' she said lightly, 'it's just that strangers might be upset if they saw my scar.'

It was a stunning idea, intimating possibilities I had never considered and couldn't begin to formulate. It must have been my first-ever glimpse of a world that allowed having a cancerous breast cut off the slightest emotional meaning.

For a long time, our mother seemed to be well again. I'm not sure how aware I was when this began to change, or whether we'd been warned that it might happen, and had been waiting all along. But two and a half years after her mastectomy, the cancer had spread from her breast to her lung, and was inoperable.

The lists were limitless. First of all, a cooking rota was drawn up, allocating each of us a night of the week to make supper, assisted by a meal plan compiled by our mother. The menus were heartbreakingly basic, but she had left nothing to chance; how to make mashed potato and grated cheese could run to several pages. In the evenings, she would sit propped up by pillows in bed, surrounded by paper-work, compiling intricate guidelines for every eventuality. Some of her lists addressed mundane practicalities: what to buy for the weekly shop, when to see the dentist. Then there were the one-off categories: who to send Christmas cards to, where to buy birthday presents. Page by page, the anatomy of her entire life was broken down into series of meticulous instructions.

There were also lists for the life she wouldn't see and would have to guess at. There were her notes on hypo-thetical motherhood, anticipating needs of teenagers she would never know, and so by necessity they were endlessly contingent; if such-and-such were to happen to her second son, say, then so-and-so might be a good person to ask for help, and so on. She worried about the novels we might not read, and drew up a list of recommendations for each child, with a suggested age at which each might best be introduced. She thought I would like E. M. Forster. She was right.

When I think about those lists now, they remind me of those artist's impressions the police produce to show how they imagine a missing child might look a decade after their disappearance. Her friends must have found them unbearably poignant, but what they communicated to a child was the very opposite of sad. As far as I could gather, if you knew how to make lists, death wasn't a catastrophe at all. It wasn't even a tragedy. It was an organisational challenge: if we organised ourselves properly, the possibility of loss could be eliminated altogether. It was just a question of reconfiguration; of restructuring a family of six into five, making sure no gaps would be left after she was gone. As long as we kept on top of the problem, there was no need to feel sad – for what was death, in the face of a thoroughly thought-out plan?

The material fact that our mother was dying was discussed every day, everywhere. The houses of our parents' friends were as much a home to us as our own, for our mother had always felt uneasy about the nuclear family, with its tendency towards secretive isolation, and had spent the Seventies developing a de facto extended version. Now it was organised into a kind of committee for bereavement, intimately and openly involved in the process of her death. She seemed to be fearless, addressing every dimension with academic rigour, and I remember how much everyone admired her courage.

But I don't remember talking to anyone about how it felt to watch her dying. It would have been unspeakably disloyal in the face of so much constructive resolve. Everything was being arranged, so I couldn't see anything useful to say.

When our mother first fell ill, it was naturally understood that information about her illness would be shared
with all of us. The nature of cancer was carefully explained,
as was the likely course of her gradual decline. We were
warned that the man who delivered her oxygen tanks to
the house had an unnerving tendency to drop to his knees
and pray at her bedside, and that we weren't to laugh or be
alarmed. She explained that were one of us to argue with
her, and she were to die that night, we weren't to feel guilty
or worry about it.

After she had died, we might imagine that we saw her,
or heard her voice, but that was quite normal, and nothing
to fear. It was possible, too, that someone who didn't know
might phone and ask to speak to her. If that happened, we
could just hand the phone to our father.

So well prepared were we for these eventualities that
when none materialised, I think I felt mildly disappointed.
The narrative of tragedy taking place in our home, as
our mother grew sicker, had been superseded by a meta-
narrative about the triumph of knowledge over fear. We
were led to understand that some families kept terminal
illness a secret, their children deceived into thinking the
dying parent would get better. But we were blessed with
the truth, and the implication seemed to be that we therefore had nothing to fear. Information would conquer all.

Even as she slipped closer towards death, I found it
almost impossible to believe something terrible was happening. How could it be, when the consensus was that we
were managing so well? As the months passed she grew

weaker and weaker, eventually no longer able to leave her room. We used to go to her one by one at bedtime to say goodnight, but I don't know whether she lay there for days or months at the end. A few years ago I was surprised to hear Matt recall the sound of her coughing ceaselessly through the night. I have no memory of it.

I can remember the night she died. It was a week before I was going to be ten, and she was lying in her dressing gown, leaning against a pillow. I must have been aware her death was imminent, because when she rummaged around for something in her handbag, I said, 'I can't really believe you're about to die.' It was more than I could comprehend – the proximity of death to something as mundane as rummaging.

'I tried to get up today,' she said. 'I tried to walk to the window.' It was about a yard from the bed. 'And I couldn't.'

'I hope you don't die on my birthday,' I said.

It seems such an incredible thing to have said that sometimes I think I must have invented it. But I can hear the sound of my voice – so brittle and breezy – and I know it is true. I think she smiled, and agreed it would be terrible timing.

I knew she had died the next morning when I woke to the sound of Ben crying. His room was next to mine, and soon my father appeared in my doorway, choking the words out through his tears. He asked if I wanted to see her, and we went together to the bedroom. She looked as though she was only sleeping. I wasn't sure if I wanted to touch her, but he said she wouldn't feel strange. She was wearing Indian slipper socks, and through the leather and wool I squeezed her toes.

I heard Tom and Matt's cries along the corridor as one and then the last received the news. Later we walked together up the valley. It was a clear February Sunday, and while we were out some relatives came to look at her body. I remember feeling angry with them, but didn't know why. I think her body was taken away that evening, and the following morning we all went to school.

Everyone seemed to know she had died. Cards began arriving, a stream of handwritten tributes to our mother. A letter came from an elderly relative, addressed to the four children, telling us to concentrate on how lucky we were to have had her for our mother. It was only when I came across the letter years later that it struck me as an extraordinary thing to tell children on the day their mother died.

Her funeral took place three days later. It was a secular service, conducted in the local village cemetery by a man from the Humanist Society. I wasn't sure what to wear. Black belonged to the world of people who said 'waterworks', but someone suggested I wear something that meant something to me, and I was floored. Clothes didn't mean anything to me; they were just what my brothers had grown out of. After the funeral we all went back to the house of friends in Long Dean, and I ate too much of my grandmother's lemon cake. In my memory it is a weirdly festive occasion.

I made up a game that spring, and used to play it over

and over in my head. What would I give, in exchange for having her back? Would I spend a year in prison? Five years? Lose one of my legs? My forfeits strike me as curiously modest now, but I took the deal very seriously, and the mental negotiations went on for months. Their conclusion came as a blinding shock. I was cycling down the lane past the dairy one afternoon, happily absorbed in the game, when suddenly it hit me. There was no deal. I could offer what I liked, but she wasn't coming back.

In the early days after her death, our family made awkward attempts at ceremony. The five of us planted a tree for her in the valley, and there were visits to the grave. But these were painfully self-conscious, and as time passed I noticed we mentioned her name less and less at home. Each of us retreated into private grief – to protect ourselves as much as each other, I think. I couldn't bear to see my father cry, and would do anything to prevent it.

People outside the family no longer cried in front of me, either. At the funeral, all the grown-ups had wept, but I saw no more tears after that, and although their intention must have been to spare me, the embargo on grief had a profound unintended consequence. It was plain to see that nobody was crying any more. There had to be a reason for this – and to me, the logic was obvious. If nobody was crying, there was nothing to cry about. And if there was nothing to cry about, then I should work out how to stop feeling sad.

By the time I started secondary school, I had come to regard having a dead mother as a piece of extraordinary good fortune. I studied other people's mothers, and couldn't believe my luck to be spared this interfering meddler. What an insufferable intrusion a mother looked like – all that driving her children about, cooking their food, taking them shopping, choosing their clothes. I couldn't think how they could stand it. Our motherless family looked by comparison a model of enviable freedom, in which each of us took care of ourselves.

This new way of looking at life was made easier to adopt by the fact that I was finding it more and more difficult to remember my mother. When anyone dies, the bereaved take comfort in a degree of posthumous deification. When someone dies young, the revisionism can get completely out of hand. In no time at all, the woman grown-ups described when remembering my mother had turned into a total stranger – a fairy-tale creature of mythical virtue. Old women would stop me in the village shop, and grip my hand. 'Your mother – your mother was an *angel*.'

The deification, rather like a video recorder, taped over my own memories until they were all gone, and replaced them with a memorial to somebody else altogether. I could hardly miss someone I didn't even know, so it became increasingly implausible to regard myself as bereaved. If I found myself feeling inexplicably sad, I would think about everyone else's loss, and feel terribly sympathetic.

Secretly, I wasn't sure I even liked this woman. After she died, her friends and relatives published a booklet of recollections, from her school days all the way through to a poem about her funeral. They called it 'An Appreciation', and must have thought it would be a comfort to her children. My copy lived beside my bed. I studied its contents compulsively, but it was anything but a comforting read, and in my heart dark resentment began to grow.

My mother's exceptional qualities of empathy and compassion had apparently been evident to all by the time she was five years old. Her school career was distinguished by a stellar combination of academic genius and social popularity, and everyone agreed she could have been a cabinet minister at the very least, had it not been for the supernatural selflessness of her devotion to children. Even death had turned to triumph in her hands. A friend wrote, 'She has given us a model of how to die.' I searched for any chink – a glimmer of deficiency – but in vain. The superlatives covered every conceivable category of personal application.

The deadliest sentence of all was a line her father had written. His daughter, he wrote, was 'a person who gave us a standard of human achievement that can serve to inspire our own conduct, and by reference to which we can measure the quality of our own lives'. He cannot have guessed the effect his words would have, but they scorched themselves onto my conscience. I interpreted them as a literal injunction, and it determined the role my mother was to play for the next twenty years. She was a rival – a formidable, ghostly rival – and the hopelessness of ever emulating her was equalled only by the imperative to try. No aspect of lovability could be neglected, I now saw, if I hoped to stay in the running.

Combining academic excellence with social success was a challenge at the local comprehensive. Popularity lived towards the lower end of the socioeconomic scale, around girls from the estates who knew about mascara, whereas I had a stupidly posh voice and the vocabulary of an undergraduate. I also had second-hand clothes, complete ignorance of the television schedules and no idea how to dance.

Another essential component of perfection, I inferred, was personal autonomy. Our father was a single parent of four, and his interest in our self-sufficiency was so transparent that I would have sooner died than let him down. When my periods began, I didn't bother to mention it. I knew what to do, so what was there to say? On my birthday he would issue me with a budget, I would buy my presents from him, and he would reimburse me. I'm not sure if he wrapped them up or left that to me. Minor illnesses or upsets were best kept to oneself, and though the mysteries of teenage fashion thoroughly unnerved me, I saw off the approaches of a sympathetic aunt with lofty scorn.

It was hard to feel love for my mother when she was such a fearful rival – but how could I hate her? Hate would be a symptom of failure – one to which my mother, with her legendary capacity for love, would presumably never have succumbed. The only target of angry frustration would have to be myself – and it fuelled the relentless self-improvement drive that I substituted for childhood.

Very occasionally, I would risk the thought that my mother had enjoyed an unfair advantage by not losing her own mother at nine, and perhaps this entitled me to some allowances. But nobody else suggested this, so the answer appeared to be no. In a sense, the situation made for a happy coincidence of desires. The grown-ups all wanted me to be fine, so they were enthusiastic witnesses for evidence to that effect. I wanted to appear as brilliant as my mother, so concealed any evidence to the contrary.

I tried so hard through my teens to evoke my mother's warmth. But losing a parent, and deciding not to mind, can cauterise your senses and make you dangerously cold. Your contemporaries seem weak and needy, their problems pitifully trivial, and you find yourself exiled beyond the reach of empathy. People who undergo an intense narcotic experience at an early age sometimes describe feeling as if their entire sensory perception has been repositioned, their perspective for ever altered. Something of that sort had happened to me.

When I grew up and left home, new friends would learn at some point that my mother was dead, but nobody asked questions. I wasn't aware of deterring them deliberately – but evidently something was communicated to put people off, and it worked. I never used to give it a thought. Looking back now, I imagine what they sensed was a stony refusal to allow the matter a moment's significance.

When the funeral is behind us, I try do something similar with Tony's death. Unless I am uniquely unlike everyone who has ever been bereaved, I say to myself, there will come a point when I can accept it. Why not just short-circuit the process, fast-forward to feeling philosophical, and spare myself the pain? Only, it turns out that I can't. I keep trying to reason with my emotions, but they aren't listening.

For the first time in my life, I am at their mercy. It is terrifying. I am a total amateur at feeling sad, and have no idea how to control the constant flashbacks in my mind to the beach and Tony's body. Sometimes the flashbacks aren't even true; I keep picturing myself pulling Jake unconscious from the water, frantically trying to revive him, and am pitched into hysterical panic over something that did not even happen.

I hate my new defencelessness, and cannot stand feeling out of control. A part of me longs to magic my old self back. But even if I could, I'm not sure that I would. If I decide not to mind that Tony has died, my children will have to as well. They will learn to dissociate from all inconvenient emotions, and I know how efficiently this would protect them. But I also know the price they would have to pay.

My family organised a system of bereavement in which anything as chaotic as anguish could be reasoned away. We held ourselves together, congratulating ourselves on our superior analysis of death, as if grief were a form of obesity or debt – a shamefully irrational lapse of self-control. We imagined we were sparing ourselves the indignity of emotional commotion, and didn't realise that, without it, recovery is for ever deferred, leaving you suspended in a state of pressure.

Sooner or later something, something had to give. At the age of thirty-one I became severely depressed, to the point where I was briefly hospitalised. It was a frightening episode, but also illuminating, for I began to reappraise the rational attitude to death we had devised, and saw for the first time the awful aridity of its brilliant self-delusion. It is a middle-class fallacy that if only you're clever enough, you can find a way to save yourself from common misery. We thought we were better than people who lived by bourgeois conventions such as 'Never speak ill of the dead'. But when did we ever speak ill of the dead? We just phrased the pro- hibition differently, and published a booklet called 'An Appreciation'. We tried to be meticulously honest with information, but the facts we faced were only those we could find a way to intellectualise.

Our mother told us everything about her mastectomy, except that it devastated her, and everything about dying, except that it would break our hearts. She couldn't tell the unbearable truth that her death was a disaster from which none of us would fully recover, no matter how many lists she wrote. It never occurred to me back then that anything was being left unsaid. I took what I saw at face value. But the conclusion to which it led me was a fatal misunder- standing – one that, had she realised, would surely have broken her heart. How could my mother have guessed what a child would make of the equanimity with which she appeared to face death? I took it to mean only one thing. She was leaving her children for ever, and as far as I could see she really didn't mind. So I decided not to mind either.

In the depths of depression I realised that of course she had minded. She wasn't happy to abandon us, but only trying to protect us from her torment. The puzzle was that although I now understood this, I was still unable to feel much about it. It was an intellectual revelation rather than an emotional awakening, and as I recovered my old habits returned; I could still control my feelings. Tony's inability to control his used to baffle and exasperate me; his helplessness in the face of emotions seemed recklessly irrational, needlessly risky. That I am growing more like him only now when he is dead feels a cruel irony.

Jake has asked me not to cry in front of him, but as time passes I do, because I want the boys to see that sadness is not shaming. But I worry that my old habits will once again return, and if my emotional spectrum contracts to the narrow safety of its former dimensions, the boys will never learn how to be as alive as their father had dared to be. I worry that if they do not learn how to grieve, or they sense that it would be letting the side down, their sadness will metastasise into anger. I used to think I wasn't angry at all about my mother dying, but all my punishing perfectionism was really just anger redirected at myself. I do not want the boys to hate themselves.

More than anything, I worry about repeating another mistake. One of the incidents that had precipitated the depression was a discovery made quite by accident fifteen years ago, in Treasure Beach, of all places. At the heart of my mother's death, it turned out, there had been a big secret after all. The agreement had been that our father would tell us when we were old enough. Only, he forgot. As the years passed he kept meaning to, but could never find the right moment, and kept putting it off until the matter had become such a muddle in his mind that he thought he had.

The secret emerged while I was living in Jamaica, and my father came to visit. Lying in hammocks at Jake's one afternoon, I asked him about the night our mother died, and he made an oblique reference to 'the pact'. What was he talking about? 'You know, the pact.' 'What pact?' Now he was equally confused. Surely I knew. 'The pact' was coded shorthand for the secret shared by the tiny group of friends involved in my mother's suicide.

She had wanted very much to die at home. She had feared the final ravages of disease which might frighten her children and demean her dignity. So she had persuaded a medic to give her a pill that would kill her when she decided it was time to die. The night she died had been planned in advance; she chose her moment, and took her own life. It meant she knew she was saying goodbye when we said goodnight for the last time. Her closest friends had been told as well. While the four of us slept, the terrible drama of their final goodbyes was being played out in her bedroom, and when we woke next day, thinking fate had taken its course, we were quite wrong. Our father had known he would be breaking the news all along.

Our mother's support for assisted euthanasia was well known, for she had taken part in a *World in Action* documentary six months before her death, and been a powerful advocate of it. But I had taken her argument for hypothesis, never dreaming she had found the means to make it real. She had decided we were too young to be trusted with a secret that could cost the doctor who supplied the pill his liberty.

Did it matter that she had ended her own life? At first I wasn't sure. I tried to tell myself it was of little consequence, and in a literal sense it was true, for she was close to death, sparing only the unknowable horrors of the end. It didn't alter my feelings towards euthanasia – and it still doesn't. I wish it were legal, and in her circumstances I expect I would do the same. But I do not think it is possible to break a promise of truth without paying a price, and I was angry.

A lie doesn't become dangerous only with exposure; it is toxic, however well buried. I think the secret leaked in ways they could never have imagined, and that at some wordless depth all of us sensed something withheld. I wonder if it is why my brothers and I withdrew so soon into our own private sorrow.

I have thought a lot about this since Tony died. The press reports of his death precluded any possibility of lying to the boys about how he drowned, but there are other facts whose disclosure may in the future present an even greater temptation to withhold the truth.

Ever since the boys were born, I had wondered how and when we would tell them about Tony's past. When would be the right time for them to know their father used to be a criminal and a crack addict; at what point would we tell them he had been to prison? But the dilemma lay far in the future and would be faced together. Now that he is gone I am the gatekeeper of his past, in sole custody of a history the boys will never have the chance to integrate or reconcile with a father they know. Alive only in their imagination, he will always be a semi-mythical figure to them, and this has transformed what used to be a distant shared dilemma into an immediate problem for which I alone am responsible.

Disclosed too early, the revelations risk upsetting and confusing them. Left too late, they would risk devastating their fantasies of a father as a flawless hero. I can see how easily these fantasies will form. Tony gave his life to save his son, deification is inevitable – and he was a hero, it is true. But I don't want their image of their father to be a work of posthumous fiction that airbrushes out all his other truths. Nor do I want them to grow up under the pressure I suffered to live up to the impossible standards of a ghost.

It is very hard to see when the time would be right. If I tell them while they are children, and see the world in black and white, good and bad, how will they be able to comprehend the complexity of Tony? If I wait until adolescence, will they glamorise his past and be drawn to emulate it? The friends I consult all assume the boys will be inspired by the redemptive triumph of Tony's life, but I worry that the message they will take from it as teenagers is that if their dad broke the law, they can too. He got away with it; why wouldn't they? Adults understand how difficult and rare it is to turn around a life of crime and drugs; it's why they find Tony's story so inspiring. What they forget, I fear, is that we all mistake our own parents for the universal norm, and can draw the most calamitously misleading assumptions from our parents' unrepresentative example. But if I wait until Jake and Joe are adults, and sufficiently sophisticated to absorb his past without mistaking it for an indictment or a licence, I think they will be furious with me for keeping secrets, and feel betrayed.

All these thoughts make me very worried about writing this book. It will surrender my editorial control over Tony's story; everything will be irretrievably known. Jake and Joe will be too young to read it, of course – but what if an older kid taunts them in the playground, 'Did you know your dad was a gangster? Your dad was a drug addict.' If I write this book I will no longer be able to choose what and when to tell them.

In the end, that is precisely why I decide to write it. I do not want ever to lie to my children, but already I can see the truth is so fraught with dangers that the temptation to edit or withhold may become irresistible. By relinquishing control I forfeit that option, and on balance this feels like the safest thing to do.

9

My feelings about the boys in the early weeks after Tony's death shock me. I do not want to cling to Jake and Joe. There is no impulse to hold my sons tight, never out of my sight. The urgent imperative to stay alive for these tiny semi-orphans in no way galvanises me. I'm not even glad they at least have one parent left. What I wish, more than anything, is that the ocean had swallowed us all up.

The first time I say so out loud, it sounds too appalling to be true. The boys are at nursery and I am in my bedroom with my cousin Shona, sorting through Tony's paperwork, when my geriatric laptop freezes. A faulty computer is a trivial inconvenience, under the circumstances, but as the screen fades to black I bury myself under the duvet in tears, and somebody starts to howl.

'I wish we'd all fucking drowned. We should all have drowned with Tony.' I realise the noise is coming from me – and worse still, I mean it. If only we could all have drowned together, we would have been spared.

I find myself fantasising about being dead, or running away. I want to get in the car, drive out of the gate and never come back. Failing that, I wish my children could be as far away from me as possible, ideally on the other side of the world. None of the above options is available, and I do not contemplate them for a moment. What these fantasies provide is a helpful illusion of choice, while I come to terms with the unprecedented futility of thinking up ways to escape.

Perhaps this is how it feels to be a lifer in prison. When everything in your life has gone wrong, ordinarily the sensible thing to do is work out how to change it. But I can think about the untenability of this new life without Tony for as long as I like, and I am not going to come up with a viable alternative. The three of us are stuck here and no one is going anywhere, no matter how bad it gets.

Before Tony died it had been easy to be a good mum. Now I am shouty and inconsistent, joyless and volatile, and shaken by how quickly I have unravelled into the screechy stereotype of a single parent. The boys used to be companionable and considerate brothers, but have turned into mortal rivals in an exhausting Oedipal love triangle, continually competing for evidence that my love for one comes at the exclusion of the other. Joe becomes gratuitously demanding, waking me at three in the morning with

'Deh-Cah! Come here and straighten my blanket!' I can see that what they need, more than ever before or anything else, is their mum – but she has gone. All the qualities good parenting requires – energy, enthusiasm, patience, optimism – have deserted, so instead I must try to perform the part of their mother. I am not a talented actor. Jake tells me he doesn't want to see me cry, and although I know the dangers for him of this injunction if it is strictly observed, in the early days I try not to cry too much in front of him, so bath time takes for ever, because I keep having to retreat off stage to my bedroom to weep before resuming the performance.

The boys have always loved a cartoon character called Fireman Sam, and the bath now becomes a nightly stage for water-based emergency rescue role play. They cram it full of lifeboats and boathouses and figurines of firemen in diving gear, and enact elaborately inventive drowning scenarios until the water is lukewarm and their toes have turned to prunes. I learn to use the time to scan the evening's bedtime story. How could I have failed to notice until now the prevalence of drowning in children's fiction? It crops up time and again – Captain Pugwash is a serial offender – and unless briefed for what's coming I can't plan how to censor the jeopardy if it gets too much for them. Unfortunately I have forgotten all about the scene in *Peter Pan* where Captain Hook ties a young woman to a rock and waits for the tide to rise and drown her, until it unfolds before our eyes in a local theatre. As the audience around us titters and squeals Jake and Joe stiffen beside me, wide-eyed, open-mouthed.

When Peter Pan drinks poison and dies, only to spring back to life after Tinkerbell exhorts us all to close our eyes and yell 'I believe!', Joe turns to me in confusion. 'Magic can bring him back alive if we believe enough? Can it really, Decca?' My heart sinks. For months I have been on high alert for mumbo-jumbo about angels or heaven, and kept the boys well away from any idiot likely to talk nonsense about Tony watching them from the stars. The finality of death is scarcely credible even to me; Jake and Joe are still struggling with the concept. I could murder Tinkerbell.

Most of the time they seem to understand, but then one will say something that throws me. 'Can we go back to Jamaica?' Joe asks excitedly, following a shopping trip to a shoe shop. 'I want to show Tony my new Crocs.' A friend from their nursery has a birthday party on a farm, and at one point all the kids pile into a tractor trailer for a ride. There isn't room for all the parents, so a young boy sits next to me, and as we're returning across the field I point out his father waiting for him. 'There's your dad, over there.' Jake's head snaps round and he jumps to his feet, scanning the crowd. 'Tony's here? Tony's waiting? Where is he, Dec, where?'

In other ways, they become unnervingly matter-of-fact about mortality. 'I've decided,' Jake tells Joe one day, 'that anyone I don't like, I'm going to make them dead.'

'But Jakey,' Joe points out, 'you like everyone.'

'Oh yeah! I forgot.' Jake giggles. 'No, wait a minute, I don't like Ros.'

Joe nods. 'Me neither.' Ros is a little girl at nursery, and in fairness to them both rather unappealingly bovine.

'Right,' Jake says. 'Next time I see her I'm going to sink my teeth into her neck, and that will make her dead.'

'Yes!' Joe agrees, and they carry on playing.

Occasionally their confusion can be comic. As I am putting them to bed one evening, a sudden thought strikes Jake. 'Oh no,' he exclaims. 'Now Tony's dead you won't be able to have another baby.' We weren't planning on a third, but I nod and agree this is true. A moment later he brightens. 'But where did Tony keep his seeds? We could find them and still use them.' I suppose at some point we must have said something about Tony planting seed in an egg in my tummy to make him and Joe. 'Oh sweetheart,' I smile. 'This might sound funny, but they lived in his balls.'

'Really?' He looks surprised. Then: 'Oh! So have I got some seeds in mine?'

'No, not yet. You will when you're much older though.'

'Oh well that's okay then. We'll just wait till I've got some, and then we can plant mine in your tummy.' He looks rather impressed with his elegant solution.

Neither of them ever cries about Tony. They still haven't to this day. I can see that grief only makes sense if you understand what you have lost, and they don't. But if they are not going to grieve, I do want us to keep talking about Tony.

Joe asks me to tell the story of how Tony died-ed every day, but Jake still covers his ears and runs away. By chance one day I discover that he will happily talk about his dad – as long as it's only about how silly or annoying he could be. So we laugh about 'what a worrypants' Tony was, or how deafeningly loud he used to like the telly, or how hopeless he was at horse riding. When we do so in front of other people they tend to look taken aback, and I sense their confused unease. I am not surprised; it must sound wilfully disrespectful. But I remember how alienating I found grown-ups' reverent eulogies about my mum, so if gentle mockery of Tony is what Jake needs it is fine with me. Another mistake from my own childhood, however, proves more tricky to correct.

Friends in London organise a visiting system to ensure we're never alone. Jake and Joe enjoy the continually changing company, but at times it can feel a little like running a small country hotel, so it is a while before I notice that no one talks about Tony in front of them. Adults rarely ever mentioned my mum's name in my presence, let alone the fact she had died, and I had always attributed this omission to the peculiar culture of our family circle, but now see it must be universal. Who wants to talk to a three-year-old about his father's death? When I ask friends to bring up Tony around the boys they blanch. But Jake and Joe must be wondering why no one except me ever mentions the worst thing that has ever happened to them.

The urgency of the boys' needs is inexhaustible, and the effort of will required to conjure a reassuring pretence of maternal competence comes close to dismantling me.

If only the world could just stop. I long for some sort of cosmic remote control with a pause button I could press to freeze time, while I absorbed the enormity of what has happened and could reassemble something of my old self. But first there is the infrastructure of a new life without Tony to be constructed.

I hire a young woman called Charlotte who used to work at the boys' nursery to be their nanny when I return to work in the autumn, find someone who can cut the grass, and work out what's wrong with our septic tank. I empty the wardrobes of Tony's clothes and seal them away in vacuum-pack bags; I teach myself to make Yorkshire puddings, if nothing like as successfully as he used to. When the builders finish and leave it is clear that we should have pictures of Tony on the walls. I can't yet bear to look at photographs of him, but worry about what people will think if the house isn't plastered in them, and Joe is thrilled to find his father's face in every room. 'There's Tony! And there! And look, there! Tony!'

In late August the boys go away to stay with various uncles and their grandfather, and for the first time everything finally stops. I go to bed and lie in darkness for five days. When I get up and drive to Wiltshire to collect them, something has changed; as I step out of the car I am no longer acting. There is no need to pretend to be pleased to see them. The excitement is authentic.

I don't know if the boys sense the shift, but as the summer draws to an end the ruins of our family slowly reconfigure into some sort of recognisable shape. Post-operative amputees often experience phantom pain for a while, until their neuropathways familiarise themselves with their new anatomy and stop searching for the missing limb. I think something like that is beginning to happen to us.

Jake starts school in September. It is a gentle little village primary, and reminds me why we moved here; he blossoms, and is all of a sudden startlingly older than the boy Tony knew. In October he turns five, and wants a birthday party at Tubslake, with a treasure hunt and egg and spoon races and all the other games we'd played at his fourth birthday party here. To deny his request would be unforgivable. To throw a party without Tony, nevertheless, feels both terrifyingly daunting and obscurely wrong. Until I had children it had not really occurred to me that birthdays are anniversaries of births. When the day comes, it is ostensibly a great success, and I am deeply touched by all the friends and family who come along and pitch in. But the only one who was with me five years earlier is missing, and his absence makes it the loneliest party I have ever known.

It is often said that you only understand the miracle of a human life when you see a baby born, but I'm not sure that this is true. After everyone has gone home, and the boys are in bed, in the silence it strikes me that having witnessed both birth and death, I know which one taught me the meaning of life.

Seeing a life taken so effortlessly before my eyes makes it miraculous to me now that any of us are walking around alive. I had never been a big worrier about my children's safety. It wouldn't have occurred to me to panic if they were late back from nursery, or wandered off in a shop, and my more anxious friends used to drive me mad with their compulsive catastrophising. Now I wonder if they don't secretly consider Tony's death to be my punishment for not worrying enough.

Fearing I will become another hyper-vigilantly jumpy mother, I brace myself for health-and-safety alarmism – but it never comes. My only new fear about the boys' welfare is one I could not have predicted, and do not fully understand. I worry that should anything happen now to Jake or Joe, no matter how freakishly unlucky, I will be judged an unfit mother, because everyone will take a Lady Bracknell view of my careless failure to keep my family safe.

This mild paranoia probably has a lot to do with the unpleasantly public exposure of single parenthood. Two-parent families are protected by the invisible shell of a couple's private language, which makes their union impenetrable to observers. Without Tony we feel skinless – a public spectacle – defenceless against the curiosity and judgement of the watching world.

The one compensation of single parenthood I would have predicted turns out to be a misapprehension. At times the directorial autonomy used to look enviable to me, for like most couples Tony and I often disagreed about parenting methods, and like most parents I believed I was right. Now I would give anything to have him here to disagree with me, for in this new domestic dictatorship I am implicated in every single thing that goes wrong, and all my old certainties have vanished. My old delusions of omnipotence are exposed for just another self-congratulatory fantasy. Tony and I had never conformed to traditional gender roles; I was the principal breadwinner, he was enthusiastic about housework. I thought of us as largely ambidextrous parents – until in the car one day Jake starts singing a song from the film *Frozen*. 'Do you wanna build a snowman?' he warbles.

'Decca,' Joe interrupts, 'do *you* want to build a snowman?'

No. No, I do not want to build a snowman. I don't want to put up a tent, light a bonfire, build a den, teach the boys how to ride bikes, go fishing, or do any of the other things I only now realise were all Tony's department. How could I not have noticed how long this list had grown? Who is going to do these things with the boys? I see now why odious men target single mothers. We are so nakedly needy. A fully committed predator would have to be a fool to waste his time on anyone else.

It must be a measure of the power of denial that compelling evidence of our new domestic inadequacy nonetheless fails to dissuade me from buying two kittens. When Jake had been unreachably distraught in Jamaica, his sole comfort had come in the form of Minerva's two cats, and at the time I made a mental note to install some at Tubslake as soon as possible.

It is my understanding that cats are low-maintenance.

A quick search on Gumtree brings up a bonanza of adorable kitten porn, and after many happy hours spent cooing over the impossible cuteness advertised all over my computer we find the perfect pair. A boy and a girl, they are tortoiseshell and fluffy; we phone their owner, and set off in high spirits to their address.

'It smells in here,' whispers Joe doubtfully as we walk through the door, but Jake has already fallen upon the kittens, and the dreamy rapture in his expression settles the matter within seconds. There is a heart-stopping moment when their owner agrees to sell us only the boy; another woman has already come to view, and been promised first refusal on the girl. I take a deep breath, and say lightly, 'Can I have a quick word with you in the kitchen?'

'Look, I hate to do this,' I confide once out of earshot of the boys. 'But I think you should know.' As I explain why these kittens matter so much to my son, her mouth falls open and sympathetic horror fills her eyes. It's a look with which I am becoming familiar, and the temptation to exploit its currency is one I am already well aware of, and concerned to resist. But this feels to me like a morally acceptable exception, and as I see her hesitate I take her hand in mine. 'Please? Could you let us have them both? Please?' We drive home triumphant, with two kittens in a basket on the back seat. We name the girl Millie, after Minerva's cat, and the boy Calabash.

They are an unmitigated disaster. Although allegedly house-trained, neither displays any interest whatsoever in the litter trays, nor do matters improve once they are old enough to be allowed outside. It's not that they pee randomly on the floor; that would be a manageable problem. No, their preferred choice of toilet is a nice soft duvet. They pee all over every bed in the house, every day.

Duvets are laundered, pillows dry-cleaned, mattresses thrown out. The sheer volume of pee feels anatomically implausible. We institute an all-bedroom-doors-closed regime, but enforcing it with any consistency on a three- and four-year-old is laughably ambitious, and the builders are scarcely any better. I waste a fortune on the false promises of useless odour-eliminating potions, and hours in internet forums dedicated to cat lovers, more and more doubtful that my feelings about these kittens qualify me for membership of such a category, only to find that no one has a clue how to solve the problem. Nor, more mystifyingly, do most fellow sufferers appear to even mind. 'Cats, huh? Hilarious!' seems to be the general consensus.

One Sunday morning I wake up to find the kittens have snuck in and peed all over my bed while Jake, Joe and I were asleep in it. We are sodden. Downstairs a double duvet is suspended over chairs in front of the Aga, like a big downy tent, drying out from its latest consignment to the washing machine. Another is bagged up at the door in a bin liner, awaiting collection by the rubbish men. The bathtub is full of pillows soaking in the most recent and ruinous odour-remover purchase from Amazon. Frantic posters are pinned up on every bedroom door: KEEP CLOSED AT ALL TIMES!!!!!! The whole house stinks. It looks like a mad lady's home. In my head I tot up all expenses incurred since the kittens' arrival a month ago – purchase price, cat food, dry-cleaning bills, new bedding, assorted feline paraphernalia – and find the total comes to more than £1,000. Enough is enough. Even if I were willing to continue living under siege, we can't conceivably afford to. The kittens have to go.

Had anyone suggested I was the type of person who buys pets off the internet and gets rid of them when they become a nuisance, I would have laughed. I'm not laughing when I drive away from the local Blue Cross rehoming centre on Monday morning. I feel like Judas. Having been given up for adoption, Tony always had a visceral disgust for anyone who gave an animal away, and I thank God he cannot see what I have done. I'm equally glad he can't see me a week or so later, when I pull in through the gates of our local prep school. Had anyone suggested I was the type of person who considers educating her children privately, I would have been indignant. But the person I used to be wasn't lonely, or frightened of the future, nor highly suggestible.

The social possibilities presented by Jake's school playground have thus far looked limited. This had not been a significant consideration in our calculations when Tony and I were deciding to leave Hackney, but if I am going to make our new life in Kent work without him I will need to make more friends, and several old ones in London assure me that a more fertile place to look would be this prep school. Coffee mornings with aggressively well-groomed bankers' wives don't sound to me like a solution to my isolation, and I would like to think the suggestion would have been briskly dismissed, were it not for another new concern.

When Tony was alive, I never doubted our parental credentials to bring up two boys. If this was naïvely arrogant I will now never know, but the assumption no longer feels reliable. Pitched against all the pressures and temptations of their peers, will I alone be enough to fortify them with the confidence and values they will need? In my current diminished state it feels doubtful. Loyalty to lifelong political disapproval of private education might, in fact, now be recklessly irresponsible; perhaps the boys need every ounce of middle-class scaffolding they can get. 'You could apply for bursaries,' the friends point out. No longer confident of my own instincts or judgements, I am talked into visiting the prep school, 'to at least have a look'. It is mouth-wateringly spectacular, and I leave dazzled. But in the dead of night later that week my conscience takes its revenge, and the punishment is brutal.

Nightmares about Tony first began when we were still in Jamaica, and have ambushed my sleep so often that humdrum predictability has downgraded their status from trauma to tiresome inconvenience. But this is a nightmare of a different order altogether.

I dream that Tony comes back. He just walks into the kitchen one afternoon, gives me a hug and puts the kettle on. My speechless incredulity seems to amuse him; it's no big deal, he shrugs casually, smiling. He was just dead for a while, and now he's alive. 'What's been happening?' he asks. 'Did I miss anything interesting?' He makes himself a coffee and rolls a spliff.

I am horrified. He can't just come back to life; what will everyone think? We're going to be in terrible trouble. No one is going to believe this; people will think he's a fraudster. They are going to be furious, they will hate us. Thinking fast, the only solution I can see is to kill him again before anyone finds out. I dash off down the lane to the prep school, and hire the geography teacher to shoot him.

But when I return, my resolve begins to falter. Tony takes me in his arms again, and the sensation of his touch, the smell of his skin, is so intoxicatingly comforting that I stop caring how difficult this will be to explain. Every rush of love I ever felt for him is coursing through my veins at once; I am engulfed by a euphoria unlike any I have ever known. I can't wait to tell him all about his funeral, and how many people were there. We snuggle up on the sofa to look through photos of the service, and all the anecdotes and dramas make him laugh. I am delirious with joy.

When I remember about the prep-school teacher I've hired to shoot him, in a panic I race off to search up and down the lane but can't find him anywhere. I decide to go home and explain the situation to Tony; he's bound to understand, and will probably have a clever solution. I find him standing in the hall, near the front door. Just as I'm about to break the bad news the catflap rattles open, and in scuttles a tortoiseshell kitten. It's Calabash.

How did he get here? How did he find his way back?

Tony crouches down to stroke the kitten, and asks, 'So which one's this, then? Millie or Calabash?'

I turn cold. How does he know their names? For a moment he blusters and bluffs, but then, as if owning up to pocketing a lighter, admits, 'Well, okay, I didn't really die. I just pretended to. I thought it would be a bit of a laugh. But I didn't like how you gave away the kittens. So I thought I'd go and get them and bring them back.' But how did he fake his own death; how did he disappear? 'Oh, it was actually pretty easy. I got Tom to help. He was in on it all along.'

I stare, nauseous with revulsion. The man is a monster. My brother is a psychopath. And no one will believe this was pulled off without my complicity. If Tom was in on the plot, I had to be too. I will be defined for ever by the grotesque celebrity of disgrace; Jake and Joe will be taken away from me, and never want to see me again.

Where the hell is that geography teacher? But he never shows up; he is not coming. I am going to have to stick by Tony's story, and tell the world he really did die and has now – it's a miracle! – come back to life. I will have to look like the happiest woman in the world. And because I can hardly then leave him, I am stuck here for the rest of my life.

I wake with a jolt, drenched in sweat and trembling. I search the bed and scan the bedroom. Where is he? I try the bathroom. By now the lights are on, I am wide awake. But it is fully half an hour before reality reasserts itself convincingly enough to discredit the dream. I sit on the bed and weep with relief that he is not alive. I weep for the obscenity of being glad he is still dead. But the bitterest tears I weep are for the loss of what I had felt in his arms.

Jake is having nightmares too, but won't talk about them, and the cool dexterity of his evasions troubles me. One day I ask if he ever talks about Tony at school.

'No, never.' Why not, I ask. 'Because everyone would laugh.' His tone is inscrutably glib. Does he mean they would laugh if he simply mentioned Tony, or would laugh at the fact he is dead? 'That he's dead.' Mirroring his airiness, I smile and ask why.

'Because when Lulu did a fart, everyone laughed. And I did too, Dec. I laughed too.'

'Well, farts can be quite funny,' I agree. 'But I'm not sure they would laugh about Tony dying. I've told quite a few children he's dead' – I offer a few names – 'and none of them laughed.' But this makes no discernible impression. He shakes his head firmly. 'Everyone in my class would.'

His emphatic hostility towards the ocean is reiterated regularly. 'I'm never ever going in the sea again,' he will calmly announce, apropos of nothing, and I take this to mean he no longer blames himself, until the day when a much older boy from school comes home with us for a play-date. As we are parking outside Tubslake the boy points to Tony's car. 'Whose is that?' I tell him it belonged to Jake's dad, and see from his look that he knows Tony died.

'I made him dead,' Jake says abruptly. His expression is as blank as his tone. 'He's dead because of me. I walked into the sea, and that's what made him dead.'

The boy studies Jake in amazement. 'No, Jake, that's not right, you mustn't think that. He was your dad, he wanted to look after you.' Jake is impervious. 'No, it's my fault, I made him dead.'

Later I ask if this is what he has been thinking all this time. Has he forgotten what we talked about – that it was the sea's fault, not his? 'No, I haven't forgotten. I did think that for a while. But then I remembered it was my fault.'

As the end of the year draws near, there are further milestones to navigate. Jake's school has a Halloween disco, and both boys want to go, so when tickets go on sale in the playground I ask for a family ticket. 'We're not a family,' Jake corrects me. 'We're not a proper family. Not now Tony's dead.' To my relief, the boys take the ghoulish festival of skeletons in their stride; they have been curious about what is happening to Tony's body in the ground ('Would he bleed if I jumped on him?' Joe asks) but appear to make no connection with the luminous skulls and zombie outfits everywhere.

I have dreaded Guy Fawkes night, afraid the boys will want another bonfire party at Tubslake. Tony always had a boyish excitement about pyrotechnics, and the previous year our field had been filled with children twirling sparklers around a bonfire so enormous no one dared go near it, and he had to find a blowtorch to toast the marshmallows. It is another relief when no party request comes. My return to work, on the other hand, presents an altogether bigger problem.

It used to feel faintly fraudulent to describe myself as a 'working mum', because whereas most husbands of my acquaintance who call themselves feminists don't know how to operate their own dishwasher, Tony could whip up a Sunday roast in his sleep while cleaning the fridge and bathing the boys. I used to fly off for days without a thought for domesticity. In fact, he made my job so easy that I was oblivious to how frequently it took me away from home. Within a week of my return to work, the household begins to fall apart.

Charlotte the nanny fields an unmanageable blizzard of emergency phone calls from train-station platforms as my schedule keeps changing, and I find myself engineering a frantic patchwork of overnight childcare from different hotel rooms; neighbours, nursery mums, the cleaner, even the decorator are all roped in, but the boys cannot keep waking up to someone new. Their regression to tearful clinginess and volcanic outbursts is sudden and shocking. When Jake's school and Joe's nursery report that they have both been wetting themselves, I am forced to concede that this isn't going to work. I will have to advertise for someone to live with us.

As job applications and CVs begin arriving, it quickly becomes clear that we are nothing like the type of family who employs a live-in nanny housekeeper. Army colonels and QCs feature prominently among the names of referees, and once the interview process begins it becomes equally clear that anyone who has chosen to make this position their profession is not someone I want to live with. The experienced ones are either ominously starchy or eccentric, while the younger candidates are sweet and charming but inspire little confidence in their being equal to unblocking a toilet. One or two trigger no obvious alarm bells, but are so stupefyingly bland that our very identity – or at least my vanity – feels imperilled. Is this what we have come to? Are we really going to wake up on a Sunday morning with someone who cites 'shopping and surfing the internet' as her preferred choice of pastime?

Salvation comes in the unlikeliest of forms. Michelle is a firefighter by profession, grew up on a Native American reserve, has a foxy South African girlfriend called Amba, and has never been a nanny or a housekeeper. After twenty years in the emergency services she is ready for a change. Elfin, quiffed and androgynous to the point Jake has to ask if she is a boy or a girl, were Michelle to be cast in *EastEnders* viewers would complain about lesbian stereotyping. We fall for them on the spot. When Charlotte leaves to go travelling in the new year, Michelle and Amba will move in. Our new domestic set-up will probably raise some eyebrows in Jake's playground, but I know Tony would have approved.

Before then we must get through Christmas. Frightened of being left alone to manufacture a charade of festivity, I formulate an itinerary that looks promising on paper, and might indeed have been fun, had Jake and Joe been at least ten years older than they are. We set off on Christmas Eve to Jenni's house in the Cotswolds, and by the time we reach my dad's the day after Boxing Day the boys are already disoriented and fractious, addled by sugar and the carousel of unfamiliar beds and faces. We plough on to Matt's house in Gloucestershire, tempers fraying from the relentless battle to keep them on their best behaviour, and on again to friends in Somerset for a new year's eve party.

I used to feel sorry for Jehovah's Witnesses, but as we limp home to Kent I am beginning to think they might be onto something after all. Signing up to peddle the *Watchtower* would be a radical solution, but I am dreading next December already, and open to anything that would provide an excuse to cancel Christmas.

There is a more urgent problem confronting us, however, and one considerably more serious. With the loss of Tony's income, and the new expense of a nanny, we are structurally insolvent – and his will leaves us not a single penny.

10

For almost a decade, Tony had been meaning to get round to updating his will. A month before we flew to Jamaica he even got as far as our local solicitor's office, but the fee had been more than £300, and as he pointed out when he came home from the appointment, 'We're about to go on holiday.' He would rather save the money for Treasure Beach. 'I'll sort it out when we get back,' he said. So Tony's last will and testament is the one he made in the nineties, naming his first wife as his sole executor, and leaving everything to her.

Had I become Tony's second wife, this oversight would not have mattered; a wedding would have nullified the will. And Tony had wanted us to marry. I was the one who always said no. A piece of paper to prove we loved each other felt unimportant to me, and so by any logical cost–benefit analysis could only constitute an unnecessary risk. This was no reflection on my faith in our future, for I could not see us splitting up. But having endured the misery of divorce once, and watched my life and finances wind up in the hands of lawyers, the only way to guarantee it couldn't happen again would be not to remarry.

So indifferent was I to the legal status of our relationship, it mattered nothing to me that Tony was still technically married to his wife. He had been trying to divorce her ever since they split up, but was unwilling to pay a lawyer several thousand pounds to do something he felt confident of being quite capable of himself. 'I mean, how hard can it be?' As the years passed, the folder in his filing cabinet marked 'Divorce' grew fatter and fatter. Tony couldn't understand it. Time and again he would fill out all the forms, present the paperwork to the appointed court as instructed, and wait patiently for news to arrive in the post that he was divorced. Instead, the forms kept coming back. The reason for their rejection was never explained, and it took him years to get to the bottom of the problem.

His wedding had taken place in Las Vegas. Being dyslexic, his spelling was atrocious, and Tony had been writing 'Los Vagas'. A quick proofread by me would have been enough to rectify the error, but as with his will I mistook Tony's divorce for no concern of mine, and this misapprehension leaves me no more legally entitled than the milkman to adjudicate over his affairs. It was probably a piece of luck he died abroad, for had we been in the UK

I'm not sure I would have had sufficient authority to proceed as far as appointing an undertaker.

The implications of this bureaucratic non-status are bewildering and infinite. When the insurance for our family car expires, I cannot renew it. The car was paid for by me, but registered in Tony's name, so must sit outside the house gathering rust and mould. My travel insurance policy, whose premiums I pay, covered my whole family on holiday, and the company agrees at once to release the death benefit – only, not to me. The money must go to the executor of Tony's will, they inform me; it's the law. Credit-card companies start phoning the house when repayments are missed, and at first they ask for Mr Anthony Wilkinson. When I tell them he has died they politely hang up. But they keep calling back every day, and evidently assume I am lying, because soon the calls come late in the evening, and open with an artfully matey, 'Hiyah, can I speak to Tony?' I have no authority to instruct lawyers to make them stop.

Nothing of Tony's belongs to me. Our two London rental flats, which represented our pension and could now save us from insolvency, were in his name alone. I do not even own his clothes or photographs. By the grace of God, Tubslake is in my name – but in our newly reduced circumstances we are almost certainly going to lose it.

Our family lawyer tells me I must contest the will. He says I have no choice. I am legally obliged, he says, because when Jake and Joe turn eighteen they can sue me for failing to protect their interests. That's not going to happen,

I protest. 'How do you know?' friends point out. 'You didn't think Tony was going to drown on holiday. But he did.' So once again my life and my finances are in the hands of lawyers.

The prospect of the legal challenge makes me ill, so my brother Ben volunteers to take charge and I sign over all responsibility to him. I want nothing to do with it. But I become a probate bore to anyone who will listen, and quickly discover that at least half my friends have not made a will either. They are horrified and shaken to learn of my predicament, but such is the peculiar power of psychological resistance to the matter, I would be surprised if any has since gone to a lawyer and made a will.

It would be of little use to them if they did. When Jake and Joe were born I had made mine, and congratulated myself for doing the sensible, responsible thing. What a smug idiot I have been. Doing the responsible thing is all very well, but in this case will by definition only serve a purpose after you are dead. So what use is it to me? One's own will is not the one anyone with sense should concern themselves with. I should have frogmarched Tony back to the local solicitor in March and paid the fee myself. I am humiliated by my own stupidity.

My feelings towards Tony's culpability are more complicated. It is hard not to feel angry with him for landing us in this mess, but I don't want to be polluted by blame. And what was his carelessness, compared with mine? A couple trusts each other with their lives, and I let him die. Had he not lived so dangerously for decades this might be easier to forgive, but for him to survive so much jeopardy only to die on my watch feels like a damning indictment, and the compulsion to apologise consumes me. Every time we visit his grave I find myself sobbing helplessly, 'I'm so sorry, Tony. I'm so sorry.'

In my mind our entire relationship is undergoing a radical reappraisal. I spent so many years fixating on the quality of our romance – did he meet my emotional needs, was I fulfilled, were we right for each other? – under the misapprehension that perfectionism is a relevant romantic ideal. I think I would have expected the relationship's imperfections to have some bearing on my sense of loss, as though grief might be analogous to losing a handbag. If the bag was a cheap old thing from Primark, you would mind less than if you lost the perfect Mulberry – and the same should presumably, I would have imagined, apply to the loss of a relationship. You could always console yourself by recalling the elements you never liked.

But our shortcomings turn out to have been immaterial. There is no comfort in the memory of the ways in which we didn't work, because it wasn't the details of our partnership that mattered, but the fact of it. We had given our lives to one another, and ceased long ago to be separate individuals. We were a joint enterprise. There are plenty of things about my body with which I am not entirely happy, but no amount of minor imperfections would mitigate the horror of being sliced in two. Without Tony I am limping and bleeding, because half of me is missing.

This is not my first experience of being single. When

the label last applied to me, however, it was immaterial, for in one's early twenties everyone is essentially single, whether in a relationship or not. Only now do I understand that loneliness is not an absence of company, but of meaning. The daily details of my existence still matter enormously to Jake and Joe, but there is no longer an adult alive for whom they hold any material significance, and the sense that I have ceased to matter is more devastating than I like to admit. If I do not belong to anyone, I do not belong anywhere.

The four people with whom I shared most of my life are all gone, and they have taken my history with them. My mother died when I was nine, and my oldest friend has been ill for some years with an incurable and degenerative neurological disease which is stealing her mind and our shared memories. My ex-husband and I still see each other from time to time, and the tenderness between us remains precious, but divorce leaves an inevitable distance that will always be unbridgeable. And now Tony is dead. Unable to locate myself in any shared narrative, it is as if I no longer exist.

Now that I am no longer building a life with someone, every day has become a transitory series of discrete experiences, for with no joint archive in which to be filed as memories they are simply discarded every night. Nothing is cumulative; I have lost my past. There is no future either, because I do not dare look further ahead than the next fortnight. I exist only in the moment – but not in a good way, not in the way therapists encourage. It feels like wearing a baseball cap pulled down very low, restricting vision to a semicircle 6 inches in front of my feet.

The surprising thing about being single and lonely is the frenzy of socialising it requires. I have never had less desire for company, nor seen more of my friends; weekends have not been this hectic since I was an undergraduate. One day I happen upon an elegant explanation for this paradox, in an interview with Judith Kerr. 'The problem with being widowed is not that there's nobody to do things with,' the children's author observed. 'It's that there's nobody to do nothing with. You have to make some plan for the day, otherwise there's this shapeless emptiness.' A weekend can no longer be left to its own devices to evolve lazily, but must be exhaustively scheduled with a full programme of children's activities, and populated by an extended cast of extras. I live in terror of last-minute cancellations, so in addition must always be careful to line up a weekly Plan B of understudies. It is a full-time job. We need a social secretary.

Jake and Joe are remorselessly drilled in the etiquette of being a good host or good guest, for we are always either visiting or receiving; they can never simply be. It is a lot to ask of a three- and five-year-old, and I worry about expecting too much ('Share your toys! Did you put the loo seat down? Don't forget to say thankyouforhavingus'), but worry more about the alternative to this social merry-go-round. Left alone with them, I am afraid I can never be enough.

These weekends cannot be much fun for our friends,

for I am poor company. There is a reason why I interview people for a living – I prefer to be the one asking the questions – and the new solipsism of grief embarrasses me. The trouble with sadness is that it seldom produces anything new to say, and if I tire of hearing myself enumerate yet again the monotony of my miseries, it is safe to assume I must be boring them too. What friends feel able to talk about to me is equally problematic.

They are understandably reluctant to tell me about their own troubles. When one or two forget and begin to recount a recent drama, they quickly check themselves – 'God, I'm so sorry, how could I be complaining about anything to *you*?' – but good news must be censored too, because no one feels comfortable telling me about anything wonderful in their life. Nor do they know what to ask. No one else has been widowed at forty-three, so they feel out of their depth, unequal to my situation, and their apprehension evokes echoes of my childhood. Nobody I knew was motherless at nine, and once again no one knows what to say. Afraid of asking the wrong thing, most tend to opt for the one question I am always at a loss to answer: 'How *are* you?'

This problem only intensifies the further I stray from the safety of low-key kitchen-table conversation. I go to a friend's garden party in Hampstead, where all of the guests know about Tony's death. The party is full of clever and fascinating people, and yet almost every exchange I attempt quickly reaches the same conversational impasse. Few guests risk straying beyond the safety of small talk, and those that do soon get stuck in the no-man's-land of a harmless-looking subject that bores both of us to death, but from which we daren't escape. I go home having learnt more about pilates and Brazilian theatre than I ever wished to know, and resolve not to go to any more parties until I am no longer a social liability.

The most successful conversations are ones in which I count my blessings. I discover this quite by accident, when one of my more Pollyannaish friends comes to stay. Telling the truth about how I am feeling is, I soon see, a mistake; her expression grows increasingly aghast, and panic gathers in her eyes. 'But of course,' I divert hastily, 'it could be worse. Jake could have drowned too.' Her panic fades a fraction, so I keep going. 'And we were so lucky to have so many friends in Treasure Beach to help us.' I can see this is definitely working. 'It was amazing that my brothers and Jenni and Danielle could all fly out.' What else? 'Um, and Tony would be so proud of how the boys are coping. Yes, and what would we have done without all the support from my family? When I think about it, this whole situation could be so much worse. We're really very lucky.'

Why hadn't I thought of this before? She relaxes into a beaming smile of approval, and I bask in its warmth. Already I can picture her reporting this conversation to others – 'Isn't she brave?' – and anticipate their awed admiration. The next time I try it out, it works a treat again. I learn to reel off my blessings by rote, and it never fails to impress.

The script is not a total work of fiction. One legacy

of Tony's death that does feel like a genuine blessing is a new appreciation of the primitive power of family. Growing up in the Eighties, I must have confused the value of family with Thatcher's 'family values', for I was suspicious of people who banged on about how much they loved their family. In my head the word was always pronounced in the estuary vowels of a *Sun* editorial – 'faaah-mly' – and Mothering Sunday and Father's Day were boycotted with contempt. 'Commercial claptrap,' I would scoff snootily. In the Nineties most of my friends were gay, and often estranged from their parents. It was the era of *Friends* and *Sex and the City*, and as we pranced about in Manchester nightclubs dancing to 'We Are Family' I fully subscribed to the fashionable new orthodoxy. Having a family didn't have to mean being lumbered with actual relatives; we were perfectly at liberty to invent our own.

If I try now to imagine these months without my family, the nonchalance with which I used to take it for granted staggers me. All the other blessings I trot out when required are neither untrue nor insignificant, either – but the device still feels fundamentally fraudulent. It is gratifying to see how it makes everyone feel better, but the idea that I feel truly fortunate is farcical, and demonstrably a lie.

The least successful conversations are those that start with someone saying: 'What you should do . . .' or 'Why don't you . . . ?' How the sentence ends doesn't matter. It could be the most brilliant idea anyone has ever come up with, but the more inspired the less welcome it is. There is already so much to do. As I have neither the strength to manage half of it, nor much faith in there being any point anyway, well-intended suggestions can only compound my sense of inadequacy. 'You're so strong, you can cope,' is similarly counterproductive. I have never felt weaker in my life, so to hear that this is yet another expectation I am failing to meet only makes me feel worse. Everyone is doing their best to be helpful, and in their shoes I would be the same, but solution-based thinking is so incomprehensible to my current state of mind that they might as well be talking in Chinese.

Another thing everyone says is, 'You won't feel like this for ever.' The pain is going to ease, they assure me; in time I will start to feel better. This is half true. What actually happens, I gradually see, is that the pain becomes normal. I get used to it. It doesn't get better; it just becomes familiar. And familiarity is an extraordinarily powerful thing.

In the early days it is sobering to discover how little my capacity for motivation differs from Jake and Joe's. In order to navigate small boys through their day, a system of modest incentives must be deployed, for without rewards to sustain them through the tedium of tidying up toys, eating vegetables, brushing their teeth, the domestic routine quickly breaks down. Any parent can tell you that most upsets in a three-year-old's world can be soothed by a teaspoon of honey. I had no idea until now that the same would be true at forty-three. I used to think myself blessed with an unusually stoical work ethic, but like most of my old self-image this proves to have been wide of the mark. In order to keep going, I require teaspoons of honey too.

They used to take the form of watching telly with Tony before bed, or an affectionate text, a private smile, or the jerk chicken he used to cook. Now that there is no longer any honey – and even if there were, I doubt I could taste it – my motivation quickly runs down. Every tiny banal act of daily life becomes a monumental effort. Without the possibility of a moment's pleasure, I find I don't really want to do anything at all.

But as the months pass, I learn to live without it. To my surprise, pleasure does not have to be the point of life – nor even a significant component. My friend Jenni tells me about a new book whose central thesis states that happiness requires a balance of purpose and pleasure, and this sounds about right to me. But it is perfectly possible, I am discovering, to survive on purpose alone.

There is just one snag. My old friends in London will put up with a puritanical drag, but the same can hardly be expected of anyone I have only just met. To build a viable life we need a social network closer to home, and Tony and I had barely begun to make a start on one when he died. It had centred chiefly on the boys' nursery, and the kindness of everyone there is astonishing and humbling; the owner cleans our house, mums leave lasagnes on the doorstep, dads invite the boys on expeditions to the forest. A man from the local pub offers to cut the grass; the bar staff want to babysit. I am ashamed to admit that the debt of gratitude can sometimes feel onerous. Having had so little time to bank good will before Tony died, I am running up an overdraft that must surely soon reach its limit. I will need to make myself more appealing to the small circle we already have, and it needs to grow wider. I haven't consciously tried to make new friends since Freshers' Week, and suspect it will require me to appear fun.

How should a newly widowed woman go about this? I decide it will be easiest if I simply don't tell anyone I meet about Tony. This is partly because I don't know how to. How would one introduce his death into casual conversation; how should it be phrased? Mainly, though, it is because I cannot bear to present myself as an object of pity before phone numbers have even been exchanged, and the instant imbalance the disclosure would create must compromise any prospect of a normal friendship evolving. It also introduces another problem which I am finding oppressive and do not know how to solve. The sympathy of people I barely know confers an obligation in return to be worthy and deserving of their kindness. No one wants to feel sorry for someone who turns out to disappoint their expectations of widowhood, and by simply being myself I am afraid I may inadvertently incur resentment, which I feel too vulnerable to risk. The situation therefore requires me to appear virtuous and unobjectionable at all times, which is exhausting and, I suspect, makes me drearily bland. The only wise course of action when meeting new people must therefore be to keep quiet about Tony.

The plan comes unstuck at the very first dinner party to which I am invited. The host is a woman I knew at journalism school twenty years earlier, who moved to a nearby village with her husband and daughters several years ago. We haven't seen each other since graduation, but she had read about Tony in the local paper and been hoping our paths might cross. When we run into each other one day, and she invites me to dinner, I am touched and terribly nervous.

At first it seems to be going surprisingly well. I sit next to an actor, and we swap anecdotes about mutual acquaintances in TV. I laugh in the right places, and begin to think I can carry this off. Look at me, I think – a perfectly normal, carefree party guest. He and his wife moved down from London only a year or so before we did, and the conversation begins to get trickier when he tells me that it has been quite tough, because she lost both her elderly parents within a year of arriving here.

Competitive misfortune is not something I had factored in when forming the plan to keep quiet about Tony. It is less than six months since he drowned, so in any contest I am almost certainly going to be stuck holding the trump card. I really like this actor and his wife; already I have started to hope we become friends. Sooner or later they are going to find out about Tony, and if I say nothing and let them keep talking about their bereavement, when they do they will feel mortified and I will feel culpable.

I'm wondering what to do when his wife and the woman sitting beside her ask me if my children's father is in the picture. 'Er, well, he was when we moved here,' I flounder. The woman has recently endured a hellish divorce, and mistakes my hesitation for caustic irony. 'Oh dear,' she chuckles dryly, rolling her eyes, 'not another one.' Waiting for my witty punchline about what bastards men are, in anticipation they begin to laugh.

Oh God oh God oh God. This is too awful; I can't let it go any further. Anxious for it not to sound like a rebuke, I tell them what happened with an insane smile plastered all over my face. Their faces freeze, and my attempt at dinner-party normality comes to a juddering halt.

Another problem I had not anticipated was the anxiety a single female in married circles can provoke. Most of the time it is subtle; a mild wariness about disclosing the husband's phone number, an unavailability for children's playdates when the wife is away. Occasionally, however, it is more direct. I am in the car with the boys one afternoon when a song comes on the radio that reminds me of an old friend I'll call Nick. We went out briefly when we first met, but that was twenty years ago, and we have remained friends ever since. He was close to both Paul and then Tony, and when he married a couple of years ago I was looking forward to meeting his wife. The song makes me smile, so I give him a ring.

A woman answers. 'Hi, can I speak to Nick?' 'Who is this?' 'It's Decca.' 'Then he ain't here.' 'Oh, well could you let him know I called?' 'No, I won't.' The line goes dead.

How weird, I think; some nutter must have got hold of his phone. When I try again later, the same voice answers. 'What do you want to talk to him for?' she growls. 'I'm sorry, who am I speaking to?' 'I'm his *wife*.' 'Oh, hi, this is Decca calling for a chat. Is he there?' 'Listen, you're his past. I'm his present. So you can delete his number now, cos you ain't never speaking to him again.'

The only thing worse than women's hostility is the suspicion that even if I were after their husbands they would have nothing to fear. To raise Jake and Joe alone and keep Tubslake going, I will need to find superhuman strength – and I worry that if I pull it off it will be at the price of ever feeling like a woman again. I will become sexless, a dried-up old boot. Already I am getting fat, and can go weeks without washing my hair, because it is hard to care what I look like when Tony can't see.

Could yoga be the answer? It sounds like a good idea. Everyone I know who does yoga looks great, and they all promise it will reconnect and reawaken body and mind. So I find a yoga teacher. She comes to the house and gives lessons in the living room. I find the first three quite promising. The fourth lesson turns into an unsolicited lecture on Buddhism, the principal message of which is that my thoughts are responsible for 'every single thing' that ever happens to me, because I 'attract' events by worrying about them. Having never worried that Tony might one day drown in front of my eyes, I am doubtful that the cause of death can have been my faulty thinking. I get to my feet, tell her to leave, and my experiment with yoga ends there.

11

No one comes right out and says so, but I can tell they think I am making a big mistake. I have decided to take the boys back to Treasure Beach.

I have never subscribed to the trite fallacy of 'closure', yet most of the reasons I offer sound suspiciously like fantasies that it can be found waiting for us in Jamaica. I say I need to be back amongst the people who were present when Tony died. His death will not feel real until I do. I cannot know if the boys will ever recover their former wild fearlessness, but am certain they won't while the horror of that day remains entombed in mystery and dread. Friends listen to all of this, and nod doubtfully. I don't blame them. By any prudent risk analysis, none of it justifies the very real danger that the trip will be a traumatic disaster.

I don't like to admit the real reason why I want us to go back. Under the circumstances I can see it must sound unaccountably frivolous. We have to return before the boys' memories of Treasure Beach fade, because once it becomes just the place where Tony died they may never want to. To everyone else, Treasure Beach is just a holiday destination, but I am willing to risk putting us through hell there for a fortnight rather than risk never seeing it again. We have already lost Tony. I cannot bear to lose it too.

Plans for the trip fall into place with miraculous ease. The owners of Minerva offer us their house again, dissolving me into fresh astonishment at the generosity of these saintly strangers. Jake's school agrees to let him go a week before February's half-term. The memory of last year's desperate visit does not deter Danielle from agreeing to come with us. Charlotte, the boys' nanny, has not yet left to go travelling, and can come. Our dates coincide serendipitously with a US public holiday, allowing an old friend in New York, Nikki, to join us for a few days. In my newly superstitious way of looking at the world, I take all these to be signs that the trip is a good idea.

The day before we are due to fly I have thought of everything. The suitcases have been packed for more than a week. I have bought inflatable sharks, rubber rings, aqua shoes, armbands, and everything else I can think of to entice Jake into the water. I congratulate myself for remembering that I will be stopped at passport control because the boys and I do not share the same surname. Tony cannot write his usual letter authorising our travel, so I assemble a meticulous package of birth certificates, his death certificate, and a press cutting report of his death. When the online check-in opens twenty-four hours before departure, I am poised at the computer. Then I open my passport to type in the details, and go cold.

It expires in five months. I open Jake's; the expiry date is less than four weeks away. Jamaica will not grant entry on a passport valid for less than six months. We are not going anywhere.

I think I am going to be sick. I don't know what to do. I call the passport office and plead and weep, but it is hopeless; a new child's passport will take at least a week. In a wild panic I try to think of any Home Office ministers I know, before remembering what happened to the last home secretary caught fast-tracking passports.

How can this have happened? I am beside myself. How am I going to tell the boys we are not going to Jamaica after all; what will I say to Danielle and Charlotte and Nikki? The thought occurs that perhaps this is some sort of Freudian self-sabotage; could my subconscious self have not wanted us to go? But of course, the explanation is more mundane. Were Tony alive he would have asked if I had checked the passports. It is one of those annoyingly point-less things couples always ask each other when they travel together, and never necessary. Only, this time it was. And he wasn't here to ask.

The only option left is so absurdly far-fetched that I am almost too embarrassed to try. I email Jason at Jake's. I don't know which will make me look more foolish – forgetting to check our passports, or expecting him to do anything about it – and am just breaking the news to Charlotte that the holiday is off when my inbox pings. It's Jason. 'You're good.' He has contacted the head of immigration at Montego Bay airport, who has agreed to let us come.

Only now, I don't know. In front of Charlotte I affect giddy elation, but as soon as she leaves cold panic sets in. If anything goes wrong on this trip now, it will be because we were not meant to go. And I will be responsible. I won't be able to pretend I wasn't warned. Fate did its best to intervene to spare us, and I did not listen. Something terrible is going to happen to one of us in Jamaica, and I will regret emailing Jason for the rest of my life.

I don't believe this for a minute, obviously. Apparently, however, it is nonetheless what I think. I walk from room to room, recalling the day before we flew to Jamaica last time, marvelling at how Tony could not have known it was the last time he would ever see his home. The hubris of such innocence now feels so breathtakingly reckless that for one fleeting moment I seriously contemplate cancelling the trip.

I still haven't quite shaken off the dread when we land in Montego Bay the following evening. The boys are sleepy but high on the sugar rush of airline food and ten hours in front of tiny TV screens, and flirt wildly with the porters in the arrival hall as I queue to collect the hire car. The man in front of me is talking about some virus called chikungunya, but I am paying no attention until he turns and asks if I'm not worried too. Until now I hadn't even heard of it. It is a mosquito-borne infection currently sweeping Jamaica, apparently, and if you get unlucky can make you seriously ill for months. The man looks anxious, but I feel oddly reassured. If that is the terrible thing waiting for us here, then frankly I'm relieved.

The one good thing about Tony not being here is that we don't have to stop at the airport to buy ganja. It didn't usually take long – he even bought some from a customs officer once, and said it was the best he had ever smoked – but by this point I'm always desperate to be in Treasure Beach, and as we set off south towards the mountains through hot tropical darkness my old butterflies return, the first flickers of authentic excitement.

It is late by the time we reach the village. The lane is silent and deserted, and becomes more pothole than tarmac after we pass through Treasure Beach, until we are bumping along a track flanked by nothing but goat fields. I sense Charlotte beginning to wonder where on earth we are taking her when the white walls and wooden gates of Minerva catch in the headlights. At last we are here.

As we walk through the door, I'm afraid everybody was right. Muscle memory of excruciating misery grips my stomach as I look around at this chillingly familiar house, and I wonder if I really have made a terrible mistake. Jake and Joe shuffle inside, dazed and bleary from sleep; I watch Jake take in his surroundings, rubbing his eyes, and in his vacant expression I think I see shocked dismay. Sensing the atmosphere, Danielle and Charlotte summon a heroic performance of holiday cheer to get us through supper, and within the hour we are all in bed asleep. I don't know it yet, but this night will mark the end of what I had honestly believed would last for ever.

'Jakey, fancy coming for a walk on the beach with me?'

He glances up from the terrace, too thrilled by his reunion with Minerva's cat to notice the synthetic breeziness in my tone.

'Sure, coming.'

The last time I saw Jake on the narrow wooden steps leading from the pool down to the beach, he had been scrambling up them, tear-stained and howling. A few days after Tony died an old friend with a boat had picked us up on the beach and taken us out to Pelican Bar, a driftwood bar built on stilts out in the ocean on a sandbank. The trip was supposed to be a diversion for the boys, but had been calamitously misjudged; Jake became hysterical, hyperventilating with fright, and we had had to turn around and come back to shore. This time he takes my hand, babbling excitably about the cat, and together we walk down to the beach. It is mid-morning on our first day.

'Let's look for shells,' I suggest casually. We find pink ones and white ones, and little black and grey ones, and as we gather them into a sun hat we inch closer towards the water's edge. Then Jake spots a half-submerged rock covered in hermit crab shells that look like baby ice-cream cones. 'Look at them! Can we go rock pooling, Dec?'

The water is perfectly still as he wades in up to his

thighs. We explore the rocks, and he pokes at crabs, and after ten minutes or so turns and looks up. 'Dec can we go for a swim?' He glances down. 'I've got my vest on, see?' I take him in my arms, we glide into the sea, and moments later he is swimming ahead of me, paddling across the bay like a Labrador.

After lunch the five of us drive into the village to Jake's. In the afternoon light the terrace is heartstoppingly beautiful, and while the kids throw themselves into the pool and charge up and down the pontoon I tumble into hugs with old friends. I have pictured this scene in my mind for so long, and worried that it might be leaden with awkward grief and the shadow of shared memories. But of course, this is Jamaica, and with each new embrace there are whoops and squeals and jokes. As I introduce Charlotte to everyone I sense her registering this unfamiliar new person I am becoming before her eyes.

Everyone refers to Tony's death straight away; no one is embarrassed or unsure what to say. I have grown so accustomed to the uncertain dance of English discomfort around death that I am sometimes relieved when people pretend not to know, so they don't have to bring it up. Even with those closest to me, I can often talk for hours about his death and afterwards almost wish I hadn't, for the weight of others' helpless concern can leave me drained and empty. But here there is no burden of anxious scrutiny to bear, and no one worries about how long the Tony conversation needs to last in order to satisfy some statutory minimum of respectful acceptability. Instead it soon draws to a natural conclusion with the same reflection, observed by everyone. 'Part a' life, Dec,' they all say softly. 'Part a' life.' Because death really is a part of life here. The presumption of longevity is a first-world luxury no one in Treasure Beach takes for granted; everyone is bereaved, one way or another, and at last I am no longer the tragic curiosity.

On Frenchman's beach we go to Eggy's bar, a tatty little shack owned by one of Tony's dearest friends. Eggy is a tall and imposing middle-aged Rasta, magnificently majestic in his bearing but so sweetly gentle that the boys hurl themselves into his lap, surrendering themselves to the fold of his vast arms. To me, Eggy has always looked rather like an exquisitely carved wooden statue, but Charlotte says he reminds her of Tony, and as Joe cuddles up and plays with Eggy's hat I wonder if the boys too sense something of their father in him.

Watching them barrel up and down the beach, what is unmistakable is their delight in the physicality of these big men. The boys' world in England is populated overwhelmingly by women – teachers, nursery workers, other mums, my friends – but here there are men everywhere, and the boys bounce from one to the next, roughhousing and playfighting, intoxicated by this great carnival of masculinity. I have sensed for some time their craving for this sort of non-verbal rough and tumble, and been pathetically grateful to any relative or friend willing to roll around on the floor with them, or hoist one over his shoulder. It comes so naturally to these Jamaican men, I am not even obligated to feel grateful.

Later that night, when the boys are in bed, I take Danielle and Charlotte to the sports park. Live Saturday night football is new to Treasure Beach, and everyone has come out dressed to kill. In the breaks between games a touchline sound system blasts out reggae and dancehall; the DJ doubles as an enthusiastic if somewhat unorthodox match commentator, and after the final whistle there is a uproarious talent contest, in which one man balances a bicycle on his head, another lifts his shirt to display expert belly rolling, and some children compete in a sack race.

It is hard to pay attention when something even more eye-opening is unfolding beside me. I have been coming to Treasure Beach for twenty years, so could hardly have failed to notice the merry-go-round of romantic adventures involving local boys and female tourists. Treasure Beach is full of preposterously beautiful young men, many of whom have applied themselves to the art of the holiday romance with the sort of commitment young men in London might devote to computer games, perhaps, or skateboarding. Attentive and funny, they are irresistibly winning to a great many women who come here, and over the years the amorous melodramas have entertained me enormously.

But they have never been anything to do with us. When I first came to live here with my husband, I did have to see off a few hopeful advances from men who assumed – not unreasonably, based on previous experience – that the minor inconvenience of a husband in the picture would be no impediment. When this proved not to be the case, I was regarded for a while as something of an eccentric. But once everyone accustomed themselves to the novelty of my exemption from the romantic economy, I became socially androgynous – so much so that it had not occurred to me that bringing gorgeous young women with me, instead of Paul or Tony, might make for an altogether different kind of experience. 'At las' you bring gyal dem wit' you Decca!' an old friend applauds warmly, patting my back and laughing while we watch the football. 'Well done, respec'.' By the end of the night I am beginning to see what he means.

One of my biggest worries about coming back without Tony was whether we would know how to have fun. Left to my own devices, I am prone to forget that having fun is sometimes more important than being sensible. I hadn't factored in the impact of turning up with Danielle and Charlotte.

Charlotte lives in a chocolate-box village in Kent with her parents and sister. She looks like an eighteenth-century milkmaid, studied child development at university, is only twenty-two, and goes out with a thoroughly nice long-term boyfriend. Her last holiday was to Disneyland in Florida. Charlotte would be forgiven for finding a place like this more than a trifle unnerving.

On paper, Danielle's background might look a little edgier, having grown up on a council estate in Hackney, the eldest child to a single mum of St Lucian descent. But Danielle is the most innocently demure, cautiously self-effacing woman I know. She and Charlotte had not met before we assembled at the Gatwick check-in desk – and having witnessed the depths of my despair at close hand, neither was expecting this trip to involve fun. What happens during the following fortnight comes as a complete surprise to all of us.

Everything begins to make us laugh. The Treasure Beach boys buzz around Charlotte and Danielle, and to my astonishment Charlotte falls in love with hardcore Jamaican dancehall. Minerva's caretaker is a young man called Weedie who I have known since he was a boy, and every time he plays Vybz Cartel, Charlotte exclaims in her home counties vowels, 'I love this music!' Although Jamaican patois floors her completely – 'I can't understand a word anyone's saying!' – soon she is riding around the village on the back of Weedie's motorbike. The girls go out every night, and even when taken to the local Go Go bar return mildly shaken but elated to have clocked up another cultural adventure. Danielle is courted by a gorgeous young man who literally serenades her ('He won't stop singing at me!') and is so bowled over she takes to shouting up at the stars: 'I love this place! I feel so free!' A trip I had pictured as a form of pilgrimage is beginning to look more like Girls Gone Wild.

One night a group of old friends from the village come to supper. Afterwards someone suggests we go to a bar in a nearby village, so we pile into cars and head up into the hills. The bar is just a shack on a grassy hillside, and a karaoke stage is set up outside under the stars. Each singer is more hilariously lamentable than the last, and eventually someone suggests we all go up together and have a go ourselves.

For ten years Tony failed to talk me into karaoke. There is no way in this world I'm about to get on that stage. 'Let's do it,' Charlotte says. 'Yes!' agrees Danielle. 'Come on, Dec,' someone urges. 'Remember, yolo.'

Yolo? Oh God, yolo. You Only Live Once – that sub-adolescent acronym for the Facebook generation, popularly invoked to excuse all manner of ill-advisable behaviour. Only here, right now, it suddenly sounds like the purest philosophical wisdom. I don't know who suggests we do 'One Love' – the last time I heard it, Tony's coffin was being carried out of his funeral – but suddenly it seems like the best idea in the world, and as the others bundle onto the stage I join them.

Afterwards Charlotte and Danielle take the mics and follow up with a Lady Gaga duet, bringing the house down. Then someone thrusts a mic into my hand, and before I'm fully aware of what's happening the three of us are singing, of all things, 'Lady Marmalade'. When it's over we are laughing and reaching for more vodka when a tall man I vaguely recognise approaches. 'Good to see you,' he says. 'Las' time mi see you, you was in mourning. How di boys?' He shakes my hand warmly. As he turns away I ask my friend Balty, who was that? 'Who, dat? 'Im own dis bar. Dat di chief superintendent of police.'

Oh dear God. I have tried so hard for so long to be a good widow – to get it right, to behave correctly – and now the very policeman who dealt with Tony's death has found me drunk in a bar, singing 'Voulez-vous couchez avec moi?' And the extraordinary thing is, I no longer care.

With each passing day, the holiday gets sillier and funnier. When Nikki flies in from New York we resolve that as most Jamaicans have at least two names – their official one almost no one even knows, and the one everyone calls them by – we need street names. Nikki is Breezy, on account of breezing in and out a few days later, and Charlotte is Sandy, in theory because she hates the sand, but endorsed unanimously, I suspect, because we can all detect echoes of Olivia Newton John in *Grease*. Danielle is Queenie, for reasons no one can remember: Jake wants to be Ready, and Joe comes up with Pinky Po. I can't remember who came up with The General for me, but everyone declares it perfect.

The strangest thing is, I agree. Until Tony died I had always assumed identity to be indelible, but pity and helplessness have turned me into a meek stranger, diminished and pitifully placatory. I had never felt less like a general in my life, nor liked myself less. But with each passing day here I can sense strength returning. I am coming back to life. When I recount tales of Tony's funeral to friends – the requirement for a bouncer, the dark extortion attempt by W – what had felt like horror stories begin to assume the comic charm of anecdotes.

The new mood is contagious, and the boys sense it. 'We,' they take to announcing proudly, 'are like Crazy Wild Jamaicans' – and it is true, they are. Of all the agonies of Tony's death, to see fear contaminate our sons had been one of the hardest, and Jake's terror of water has tormented me. Tony's fear of water cost him his life; had he not floundered and gasped in panic, the swell could not have flooded his lungs. My anxiety is not that Jake might one day drown too, but that his phobia about water will infiltrate his feelings towards the world. Fear can be dangerously infectious, and I want his old boldness back.

Day by day, a little more returns. He learns to swim in the pool at Minerva, and one night he and Joe throw their own impromptu pool party, splashing about until midnight with a gang of local kids they know. They both become casually matter-of-fact about drowning. 'This is so I don't drown,' Joe tells me, pointing to his rubber ring. When Jake stubs his toe in the pool and yelps 'Ow!' Joe inquires calmly, 'Are you drowning, Jakey?'

One morning we go back to Pelican Bar, the bar built on stilts out in the ocean. Both boys say they want to, but Jake repeatedly warns me, 'I'm going to be a bit scared when we get there.' As we plane across indigo waves he stands and lowers his hand overboard, electrified by the speed and warm spray, and when he clambers off the boat up the rickety steps he turns to me in surprise. 'Oh, it isn't scary at all.' He and Joe swim in the surrounding shallows for over an hour, chasing fish and pretending to be sea monsters. The following day, when the wind picks up and the sea turns rough, we head to Frenchman's beach where the fiercest waves come crashing in. Jake used to love the ocean on days like this – 'More monster waves!' he would shriek, willing them to tumble him upside down under water – but these are powerful enough to make even Danielle and Charlotte hesitate, and as we wade into the surf my heart is in my mouth. Under protest ('But I can swim now! I don't need this baby thing'), Jake has put his floatation vest on; I have no fear for his physical safety. He plunges headfirst into the first roller and disappears, surfacing in a salty daze behind us on the sand. For an awful moment I think he is crying. But he is laughing – 'It got me, it got me! I love it' – and races back in to catch the next wave. Joe is in Charlotte's arms when a mammoth breaker spins them both into underwater somersaults, like a giant washing machine. When they eventually emerge he has been sick all over her hair, but both are shrieking with delight.

We still have not been back to Calabash beach. I don't expect the boys will want to – but one day Jason and Laura invite us to a beach barbecue at a house just around the headland from Calabash. As soon as Jake hears this he exclaims, 'That's near Calabash Cottage! Can we go back to Calabash Cottage?' Unsure that I will be able to hold myself together, I leave the boys at Minerva later that morning and drive alone to Calabash Bay.

As I reach the beach I spot Blouser cooking over an open fire beside his shack. Damian waves from the villa above, and we embrace. A group of young men from a villa along the beach are standing waist-deep in the ocean playing frisbee, no further out than Tony was when he drowned. I stare at them, envying and despising their ignorance; they have no idea what happened here, and if they did I doubt they would believe it. I can barely believe it myself. The geometry defies reason, the distances are too tiny. How could this placid little corner of the bay, no bigger than an average garden lawn, have stolen a man's life? I thought that coming back would make what happened real to me, but I was wrong.

I do not cry or come undone. I feel quite calm. At first I think this must be numbness again – but as I sit and gaze out to sea realise it isn't that at all. The sensation is so unfamiliar, it takes a moment or two to identify. It is peace. I feel closer to Tony here, where he drew his last breath, than I have at any moment since he died.

When I return to Calabash with the others, Charlotte is stunned. The innocent tranquillity is so unlike the picture she has carried in her mind that she simply cannot comprehend how this can be where Tony drowned. Danielle breaks down, and has to go back to the car. But the boys race up and down the beach carelessly, waving up to Calabash Cottage and clambering over fishing boats, as if oblivious to the significance of this spot. Only when I ask if they would like to swim does Jake's expression tense. 'No,' he says quietly. 'Let's swim at Minerva.'

The sun is hovering just above the horizon when we reach Minerva, and the five of us swim out into the bay to watch it set. As it sinks from view, bruising the sky pink and purple, I am struck by the date. It is the 15th of February – nine months to the day since Tony died. They have been the longest nine months of my life. But the misery that felt as if it would imprison us for ever has lifted; here we are, the very same people who stumbled into this house nine months ago, dismantled by grief, and now

everything is different. Whatever happens now, and whoever we become, we are no longer those broken ghosts. I
turn to look at Jake and Joe's heads bobbing in the water,
and for the first time we feel like a family again.

Acknowledgements

A list of all the people who have helped since Tony died would be longer than this book. Their generosity and love has been astonishing, and humbling. Where my children and I would now be without them, I do not know.

But I do know that without three of them, this book would not exist. To Jenni, Johann and Natasha, my gratitude is limitless and everlasting. Thank you.